The Art of
DORA
CARRINGTON

The Art of
DORA
CARRINGTON

Jane Hill

Foreword by Michael Holroyd

Thames and Hudson

First published in Great Britain in 1994
by The Herbert Press Ltd.

First published in the United States of America
in hardcover in 1994 by Thames and Hudson Inc.,
500 Fifth Avenue, New York, New York 10110

First paperback edition 1995

Library of Congress Catalog Card Number 93–61838
ISBN 0–500–27857–1

House editor: Julia MacKenzie
Designed by Pauline Harrison

Printed and bound in Hong Kong

Contents

Acknowledgements 6
Foreword 7

London 1910–1914
1 The Slade Years of Apprenticeship 11

Hurstbourne Tarrant 1914–1917
2 Own Voice 25
3 The Modern Movement. Black and White 35

Tidmarsh Mill 1917–1924
4 At Home – People and Place Portraiture 47
5 The English Tradition of Popular Art 65
6 An Expanding World – At Home and Abroad 81

Ham Spray 1924–1932
7 A Green World – Conversation Pieces 91
8 Vanitas. Fugitive Light 111

Conclusion – Time and Tide Wait for No Man 131

Notes 134
Chronology 138
Index 140

To Andrea, for having faith

ACKNOWLEDGEMENTS

This has been a long project, greatly assisted by the goodwill I have met with all round. Limited space prohibits me mentioning all those who have been so generous with their time and memories, but my heartfelt thanks go to each one. In particular, I would like to thank the Carrington family for their patience and early guidance: Catharine and the late Noel Carrington, and their daughters, Joanna Mason and Jane Carrington. Frances Partridge has been gracious and responsive from the first and I would like to thank her for permission to quote from Carrington's unpublished letters and diaries, from *Julia: A Portrait of Julia Strachey by Herself and Frances Partridge*, and to reproduce paintings and photographs in her possession. I am grateful to several institutions and their staff: the Slade archivist Stephen Chaplin; Sally Brown at the British Library; the Lytton Strachey Trust; the Tate Gallery Archive; and the Harry Ransom Humanities Research Center at the University of Texas at Austin. I am indebted to the Authors' Foundation and the Acland Edwards Trust for essential practical support, and thank my editor Julia MacKenzie both for her contribution and for being so nice to work with.

Some people have been involved with this book from the beginning and I owe them a personal debt: Margaret Brookes for introducing me to Carrington; Teresa Grimes, who generously shared material when we were working on the same subject; Michael Holroyd for his encouragement; Rych Mills for a constant flow of material from Canada; Jane Wynborne for the extended use of her car; Peigi Angus for the loan of Higgins House; Susie Honeyman, Ginny Perkins, Catherine Rickman, Renato Lusardi and Andrew Douglas for their continuing interest; Marybeth Hamilton for our breakfast-time discussions; Robin Kinross for his sound judgement; Clive Boursnell for his unflagging support; Richard Warholic for being an inspiration to me; and my mother, Joyce Hill, for always being there.

I am grateful to the individuals and publishers who have kindly granted me permission to quote from copyright material, in particular Jonathan Cape Ltd and the estate of Dora Carrington for permission to quote from *Carrington: Letters and Extracts from her Diaries*; Richard Garnett for permission to quote from the letters and books of David Garnett; Luke Gertler for permission to quote from the letters of Mark Gertler; Michael Holroyd for permission to quote from *Lytton Strachey: A Biography*; Lady Pansy Lamb for permission to quote from the letters of Henry Lamb; John Murray Ltd for permission to quote from *A Life of Dora Carrington 1893–1932* by Gretchen Gerzina; Sinclair-Stevenson Ltd for permission to quote from *The Interior Castle: A Life of Gerald Brenan* by Jonathan Gathorne-Hardy; Thames and Hudson Ltd for permission to quote from *Carrington: Paintings, Drawings and Decorations* by Noel Carrington.

NOTE

Carrington's spelling and punctuation were erratic. These have been retained in places where they highlight Carrington's wit and character, but elsewhere they have been corrected.

Dimensions of the pictures are given in centimetres followed by inches, height before width.

Foreword
by Michael Holroyd

Carrington, who died in 1932 eighteen days before her thirty-ninth birthday, did not become known to the general public until the end of the 1960s. The first retrospective exhibition of her work was opened at the Upper Grosvenor Galleries in London in 1970 by the Arts Minister, Lord Eccles, who languidly referred to her as a Sunday painter – at which moment there was a spirited protest from Duncan Grant, followed by a growl of support from the spectators. For we could all see from the catalogue that Carrington was a professionally trained artist, a scholar of the Slade School of Fine Art where she had won several major prizes. Besides, all round us, crowded almost haphazardly on the walls, was the glowing evidence of her lifelong and passionate involvement with nature and human nature.

The same year, David Garnett's *Carrington: Letters and Extracts from her Diaries*, was published. As Jane Hill reminds us, Carrington used to write 'vivid, painterly, illuminated letters' which may have robbed her of painting time but which gave her many ideas for pictures. Until then no one but the recipients had felt the magical charm of this correspondence which, Virginia Woolf had assured her, was 'completely unlike anything else in the habitable globe'.

For a long time the figure of Carrington had floated ghostlike and half-concealed behind a number of minor fictional characters. She was Minette Darrington in D.H. Lawrence's *Women in Love*, and Mary Bracegirdle in Aldous Huxley's *Crome Yellow*; the doll-woman Betty Blyth in Wyndham Lewis's *The Apes of God*, and the painter-photographer Anna Cory in Rosamond Lehmann's *The Weather in the Streets*. Nearly forty years after her death, she was emerging from the cover of these creations into her own territory. People began to look at some of her pictures and read some of her letters, learning of the curious life she led with Lytton Strachey and of her suicide after his death. The fascination she held for those who had known her began to seed itself in the imagination of a new generation.

This fascination, and the means of tracing many of her paintings which the Upper Grosvenor Galleries had provided, led to a second exhibition of her work at the Christ Church Picture Gallery in Oxford, timed to coincide with the publication of her brother Noel Carrington's pioneering work, *Carrington. Paintings, Drawings and Decorations* in 1978. In his Foreword to this book, Sir John Rothenstein recorded that during his period as Director of the Tate Gallery from 1938 to 1964, he had never been shown an example of her work or heard an intelligent allusion to it.[1] When he subsequently got a chance to examine the pictures, he judged her to be 'the most neglected serious painter of her time'.

Jane Hill discusses the problems encountered by women painters in the early part of this century, but she also reveals Carrington's obsessional secrecy. Hardly ever did she look straight at the camera or place her work on show, so it was not surprising that she remained so long unknown. Noel Carrington described his book as a 'tardy tribute'. It was first brought out by the Oxford Polytechnic Press and two years later, in 1980, taken over and reissued in a revised edition by Thames and Hudson – another sign that her years of neglect were coming to an end. Though it would certainly have astonished Carrington herself, she inevitably became the subject of feminist research designed to rescue the achievements of women that had been obscured by a predominantly male culture. During the 1980s she was to have her biography published (*A Life of Dora Carrington 1893–1932* by Gretchen Gerzina, 1989), her paintings seen on television, and several articles written about her in magazines. Then in 1993 she found a place in *Missing Persons* as one of those people whom the editors of the *Dictionary of National Biography* recognized as having been unjustly omitted from this standard reference work. The business of rediscovering Carrington was complete and it was at last possible, without special pleading, to value her accomplishments.

A cruder test of value was taking place in the galleries and auction houses. Jane Hill records that Carrington was delighted to sell a picture in 1914 for £5 8s, and that she was specially commissioned in 1920 to paint the portrait of Lady Strachey for £25. Fifty years later, at the Upper Grosvenor Galleries, I myself saved up and bought a Carrington for £15, and I remember that prices did not much exceed £25. But by the early 1990s, one or two of her rare paintings coming up for auction at Christie's were fetching £25,000.

Jane Hill's book is very well timed. It will not be the last word on Carrington – already there is a new selection of her correspondence in preparation – but it is the most thorough examination of her work we have, based on a wide range of published and unpublished sources. 'Do you know,'

Carrington wrote to Lytton Strachey in 1923, 'I am never so happy as when I can paint.' Jane Hill treats her first and foremost as a painter and, losing no time, has her registering at the Slade in the opening sentence.

Under the supervision of Brown and Tonks, and in the legendary afterglow of Augustus John, Carrington escaped from her confining Victorian home and, as part of a 'Wild Group' of students, developed her artistic outlook at the Slade. Jane Hill uses the correspondence with C. R. W. Nevinson, Mark Gertler, and later Henry Lamb to show how her painterly expectations grew. In contrast to the academic training of the Slade, there was also the influence of Roger Fry, the 'brahmin of Bloomsbury', whose revolutionary exhibition in 1910, 'Manet and the Post-Impressionists', introduced her to the work of Cézanne and Matisse. It was equivalent, Mark Gertler wrote, 'to the impact of the scientists of this age upon a simple student of Sir Isaac Newton'.

Carrington was principally an autobiographical artist who painted the people and places she loved. Jane Hill sketches in aspects of her life to help analyse and illuminate the wide diversity of her work: public-house signboards, rococo tiles, tinselled glass pictures, drawings, decorations, sketchbooks, woodcuts and illustrated letters. The two houses she shared with Lytton Strachey, the Mill House at Pangbourne and Ham Spray House near Hungerford, were like pictures inside which she lived. Jane Hill recreates them both in marvellous detail and introduces us to the friends and lovers, men and women, who went there. We see the splendidly athletic Ralph Partridge whom she married, and his friend, the romantic Gerald Brenan whom she loved, and the seafaring Bernard Penrose whose attraction for her no one could at the time understand. We also see the women who befriended her like Lytton's sister-in-law Alix Strachey, and the women who attracted her sexually such as Lytton's niece, the novelist Julia Strachey whose husband Stephen Tomlin was also briefly one of her lovers. Her life bears witness to 'a great deal of a great many kinds of love', and a knowledge of the intensifying complications this led to enables us to look at her pictures with special intimacy and understanding.

1. The Tate now has one painting by Carrington, *Farm at Watendlath*, given by her brother Noel in 1987.

Group of Slade students and staff *c.* 1911. Front row: Carrington (extreme left), C.R.W. Nevinson (with braces), Mark Gertler (with walking stick), Stanley Spencer (second from right). Second row: Hon. Dorothy Brett (seated behind Nevinson, with velvet lapels). Back row: Professor Brown (second from right)

London 1910–1914
1 The Slade Years of Apprenticeship

When Dora Carrington came down to London in 1910, having passed her Senior Oxford Exam at Bedford High School for Girls, it was to register in the Department of Fine Arts at the Slade School of Drawing, Painting and Sculpture. Dora had shown a precocious talent for art, consistently winning, from the age of twelve, annual awards for the best school drawings as judged by The Royal Drawing Society of Great Britain and Ireland. The winners had their work exhibited in London and when Dora's art master persuaded her family that that was where Dora should go to art school, she opened the sluice gate which had been containing Dora's developing talent, and provided her with the means of escape from the life of 'conventions ... and ... taboos' in which Dora had been raised.[1]

Dora was seventeen and, to outward appearances at least, the dutiful daughter of Victorians. But in later years she would describe the horrors of home, and the awful childhood she felt she had had, writing during one of the obligatory visits she payed her mother throughout her life: 'Here I am plunged in the middle of Benares brass life, and Japanese screens ... I am too depressed by the hideousness of this house, and the bric à bracs.'[2]

Although serendipity played its part in the choice, Dora's art master could not have suggested better. With hindsight the Slade was at the most transitional and influential time in its history. The rules governing women were slackening and Dora found the liberty to give rein to her truly iconoclastic nature. Within the year, emotionally and creatively, she had established the tenets by which she would live for the rest of her life. Although the atmosphere of genteel England was still, as Virginia Woolf described, 'a perfect fossil of Victorian society', Carrington cropped her 'mothers' glory' short enough to show the furrow in the nape of her neck; began to make her own

Dora Carrington (seated second row, extreme right) at Bedford School for Girls, 1905. By kind permission of Bedford High School for Girls

unencumbered clothes; dropped her Christian name, which she considered vulgar and sentimental, and insisted on being known ever after as Carrington, *tout court*.

Set back off Gower Street – then as now a busy arterial road – in part of the west wing of a handsome neo-classical quadrangle with green lawns, the Slade was like an oasis in the midst of a bustling city. It had opened in 1871, following a bequest from Felix Slade, in accordance with his wish that the school should have its home within University College London and that it should provide an enlightened environment equal in status and achievement to the departments of arts and sciences already within UCL.

In this and other things the Slade was revolutionary. Its constitution and ethos were modelled upon the teaching methods of the French ateliers, and in particular the Parisian Salon des Refusés, which put an emphasis on working from the figure, and offered an early liberation for students from

Olivia, 1909, pen, ink and wash on paper

Carrington painting her father, Samuel, *c*. 1910

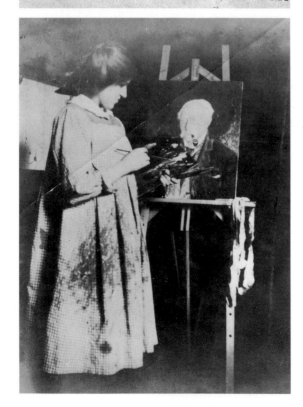

overlong working from the Antique, which the Royal Academy schools still practised.

Coming to the school in 1910 Carrington was following on from what Augustus John called 'the Grand Epoch of the Slade ... [in the 1890s when] in talent as well as looks the girls were supreme'. Women had always been part of the Slade's business, outnumbering men by two to one, but whereas for women it was seen as a kind of finishing school, for men it was a place of vocational training, reflected in the fact that Augustus not Gwen John's paintings were chosen to hang on the walls.

And the corollary of this was that if women chose a career path which did not include marriage they were considered 'unnatural'. If marriage came into their lives it was understood that they would give up painting.[3]

One of Carrington's first friends at the Slade recognized the problem facing women painters. Christopher Nevinson wrote: 'I don't want to discourage you but as you happen to be aiming high you have quite simply a bloody struggle in front of you of course not only with your actual self-expression but that vile dead wall of prejudice & hatred against a woman or still worse that superficial summing out of your work as "too clever" that so-called people of taste are addicted to ... especially [to] women [as] you lose your youth.'[4]

The teaching staff in 1910 was a catalytic combination: Frederick Brown was professor; Henry Tonks and Philip Wilson Steer his assistants; Roger Fry, the visiting lecturer in the History of Art. The four men were friends, all practising artists – giving the Slade the undoubted advantages of being a school run by artists for artists – and all members of the New English Art Club which, when it was set up in 1886 as a challenge to the conventional and more complacent Royal Academy, was the most exciting exhibiting society of its day and synonymous with the Slade which fed and watered its ranks.

There were no classes as such. The courses of study were: Drawing from the Antique and Life; Sculpture; Painting from the Antique and Life; Composition; Perspective and Lectures. Subjects for composition were given by the Professor once a month and, each summer, when school closed down for the vacations, a selection of subjects was set for the Summer Figure Composition.

The building was open six days a week from 9.30 to 5, except on Saturday when it closed at 1, and the rooms were largely unsupervised. Tuition was of the perambulatory kind with staff doing the rounds of each room at least once a day. At such times contact took place over the 'donkey' (a low-level stool with stand for drawing) and teaching was by demonstration, sketching down the margins of the drawing.

Whereas the ancients learned to draw by painting, the moderns have always learned to paint by drawing. Tonks in many ways was the embodiment of the Slade and it was Tonks who taught students very thoroughly how to draw, by the example of the old masters and an understanding of the make-up of the body, for which Tonks' training as Demonstrator of Anatomy at the London Hospital had equipped him.

Carrington produced two distinct kinds of drawings at the Slade: ones in which form and modelling were predominant and others in a linear style, where everything was made subordinate to a clear definition of outlines and interior lines.

In spite of the Slade's liberal approach to teaching art, all but the most persuasive students were expected to spend a year, often in bored sufferance, kicking their heels among the aspidistras and plaster casts of Graeco-Roman sculpture.[5] And students served their apprenticeship drawing Michelangelo's *Dying Slave* or the *Discobolus* 'until judged sufficiently advanced to draw from Life'.

One of the few consolations of the Antique Room was that it was the only studio in the school where women and men officially came together. Propriety was such that everywhere else was segregated and on the whole students were not encouraged to mix even in the corridors or on the lawns. But undoubtedly there were opportunities for the beginnings of friendships. Carrington was very soon noticed by Paul Nash who described her as: 'one of the Slade girls who was both clever and good-looking to an unusual degree … and when she cut her thick gold hair into a heavy golden bell, this, her fine blue eyes, her stutter, her turned-in toes and other rather quaint but attractive attributes combined to make her a conspicuous and popular figure.'[6]

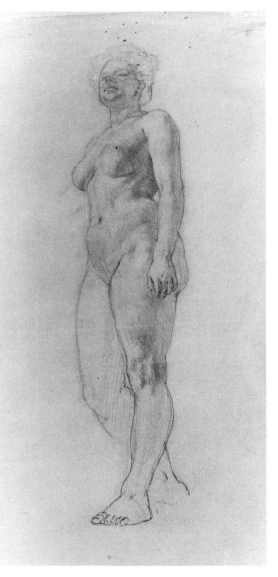

Life Drawing, 1913, pencil on paper, 50.7 × 31.7 (20 × 12). Photo: Witt Library

Carrington's confidence grew apace and she prospered. For her first year at least, her world was mostly female orientated; she was lodged in an all women's college hall in Byng Place; worked a full week and regularly on Saturdays when most did not. By the second Saturday of term she was first into the studio and taking the printed C in the attendance book for the title letter of her name. By the second term she had dropped the D for Dora and her signature had taken flight, occupying two lines and a boldly struck underline which separated it from the rest.

Carrington received her Certificate for Drawing at the end of her first year and, as soon as Professor Brown agreed, she moved into the Women's Life Room, where figure and draped models posed every day. Forty-five minute poses were set, so that the student could make fairly rapid drawings from the figure. The awards Carrington had won at school had mostly been for figure drawing and her life drawings are among the best in the Slade collection, but they also testify to the difficulties for a developing artist working within a framework which set Ingres and Leonardo da Vinci as the heights to aspire to. When one looks through the drawings from the Slade there is no clear way of distinguishing between those made by women and those made by men. They are all equally 'masculine' and commensurate with the formula of drawing which was taught.

Carrington's mature drawings of nude women would be very different and intensely erotic. But while at the Slade her life drawings were made for the purposes of instruction. In this vein Carrington's study of a woman is a very good academic drawing, if a little burdened by the lessons she was learning about modelling and perspective. One cannot help feeling that the model appears rather more Amazonian than a prod in her belly would have revealed.

Returning home to 1 Rothsay Gardens, Bedford between terms, and the iron-railing demarcations of late Victorian society, having savoured the salt of another kind of existence, cannot have been easy. Bedford was an unspoilt country market town famed for its private schools and for being the popular retiring place of ex-Empire builders. 'Though only fifty miles from London by train Bedford might have been almost a thousand for all the cultural influence then exercised on it by the

Bedford Market, c. 1911, pencil, ink and watercolour on paper, 43.2 × 66.8 (17 × 26¼). Courtesy: Anthony d'Offay Gallery, London

Souvenir of a Slade Dance, Albert Rutherston, 1912, watercolour on silk. Barbara Hiles (third from left); (l to r in right-hand group) Hon. Dorothy Brett, Carrington, Ruth Humphries. Courtesy: grandchildren of the artist

metropolis.'[7] The friends Carrington had begun to make had radically expanded her outlook and expectations of life. She had seen the new wave of art coming across the Channel from France and she had begun to read 'Tolstoy, *Tristram Shandy*, Mary Wollstonecraft, and Romain Rolland'; books that her educated brothers had never even heard of.[8]

In a spirited group of women, brought together by their will to become very good artists, Carrington found soul mates probably for the first time in her life, forming friendships with Barbara Hiles (in 1912), Ruth Humphries, Alix Sargant-Florence and the Hon. Dorothy Brett, which lasted throughout her life. Barbara had the kudos of having attended art classes in Paris on the 'Cours Libre' at the Grande Chaumière, where women and men drew and painted from the nude together. Ruth was Carrington's most intimate friend and as much a winner of prizes as Carrington. Alix was the daughter of the painter Mary Sargant-Florence. And then there was Brett, the eldest, daughter of the second Viscount Esher, who was said to be the aunty of the 'Wild Group', as they became known.

Carrington and her friends took perpetual pleasure in the look of everything, beginning with themselves. Albert Rutherston's watercolour of a *Souvenir of a Slade Dance*, 1912, pictured himself

and Augustus John supporting a cart overflowing with students and the serious supervisory figure of Tonks. The eccentrically costumed and bedizened figures of Carrington, Brett, Humphries and Hiles at the front give an indication of the vital life Carrington was living and also suggests the element of bohemianism and sophistication that John and Rutherston brought to it. Curiously enough it was a life not reflected in Carrington's own pictures of the time.

Through Nevinson, who had been raised in the spirit of internationalism by his mother, a writer and suffragette, and his father, a radical journalist, Carrington was introduced to Hampstead intellectual life. And from Mark Gertler she discovered the little Austria in Spitalfields, where the Jewish émigrés lived, absorbed into England but not integrated, where Yiddish was the first language and poverty generic.

But if she could close her eyes to the horrors of 'the ottoman and the whatnot' of provincial life, the benefit she found was in the readiness of her family to sit for her. Carrington was devoted to her father and loved to draw him.

Samuel Carrington had spent his working life in India, since the Mutiny of 1857, directing railway building for the East India Company. He was also widely travelled and had seen much of the East and America. Clearly he was unconventional,

RIGHT *Daddie and Teddie*,
1911, pencil on paper,
33 × 25.4 (13 × 10). Private
collection

OPPOSITE ABOVE Samuel
and Charlotte Carrington
at their marriage in 1888

OPPOSITE BELOW *Noel
Carrington, c.* 1910, pencil
on paper, 30.5 × 25.4
(12 × 10). Private
collection

March 29 1911

Daddie.

Teddie.

choosing not to marry until he was in his fifties, already a little 'deaf from overmuch dosing with quinine', and recently retired home to England.[9] Samuel's seemingly first and last ditch choice fell, in 1888, upon Charlotte Houghton, the sister-in-law of his niece, a woman already in her thirties and, as popular opinion would have it, past her prime. Together they had five children; two girls, three boys, of which Carrington was the fourth.

Carrington's adoration of her father, so apparent in the many drawings she made of him, polarized in her aversion towards her mother, of whom she wrote: 'she adores making a martyr of herself, toiling unnecessarily – and working off her sensual side in religious outbursts.'[10] Charlotte's demands for filial devotion and her will to subvert came to include Samuel who, through invalidity and sinking age became just as much prey to her rule as the children. Carrington captured the pathos of a typical family scene in her drawing of the family 'at music'. Charlotte is tight lipped and ladder-backed at the piano; Samuel has the air of reverie and isolation that had become his usual state; only Teddie playing the violin, through the efficacy of Carrington's line, appears relaxed.

Carrington often persuaded her brothers and their friends to sit for her. Although there were five children Carrington only ever felt an affinity with Teddie and Noel. In later years in London she crossed the street rather than speak to Lottie or Sam. Teddie, the third child, although dark, looked the way Carrington might have done had she been a boy, but Noel, the fifth child had the chiselled features of their father and Carrington drew him with a controlled, linear line.

About 1910, before she cropped her hair, Carrington made an image of her limpid-eyed, full-featured face which was utterly without vanity; penetrating and revealing to an unusual degree. Carrington would often draw the polarities of light and dark and she drew her self-portrait, with the thick strokes of a blunt lead, in the most unflattering light there is, portraying the distortions brought about on a face lit up at night by a flame. And she did it so critically her face appears almost battered, her eye sockets bruised, and it comes as some surprise that this is the face of a girl of seventeen.

As the rapid drawing of Teddie at the violin showed, Carrington had a gift for expressive line and would more generally use a linear style for drawing, as seen in *Bedford Market*, *A Cockney Picnic*, and *Dante's Inferno* (which was submitted for a Slade competition in 1911). Carrington's drawings were technically very good. *Dante's Inferno* was a model of cataclysmic hell and a perfect example of how to compose a picture.

The charm of these figure compositions lies partly in the fact that they are period pieces and we respond to them in the way that we would to the drawings of E. H. Shepard. But they have none of

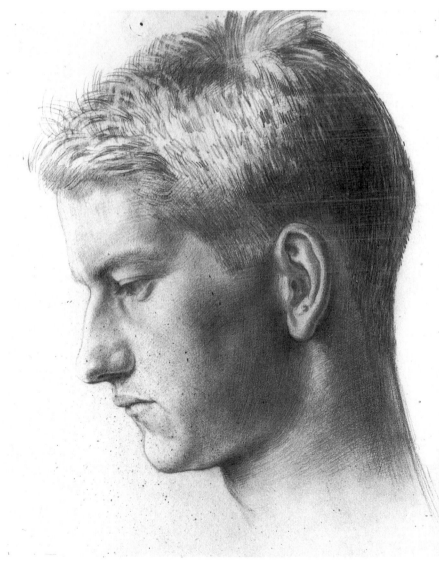

17

Self-Portrait, c. 1910, pencil on paper, 22.8 × 15.2 (9 × 6). Private collection

probity of art and that all it lacked was the tint. Painting is the primary work of the artist and Carrington was first and foremost a painter. Drawing and using watercolours were only ever preparations for painting and a means to an end. Although she always drew by line, Carrington preferred to model through paint.

Carrington was taught that the sure way to becoming an artist was through studying the work of the artists she revered. Students were encouraged to visit the national collections and libraries and to either copy directly from the paintings or to buy reproductions and to work from those. Good reproductions in colour were readily available in periodicals such as the *Burlington Magazine* and the new shilling monthly, *Colour*, which matched the Munich colour paper *Jugend*. *Colour* was the first cheap periodical dealing with modern art to offer good quality colour reproductions, and in 'Palette and Chisel' it listed new exhibitions, elections and commissions.

Through the work of art scholars such as Bernard Berenson art connoisseurship was making discoveries for the twentieth century; unearthing the work of painters, such as Stefano di Giovanni Sassetta, who had been overlooked by Giorgio Vasari in his *Lives of the Artists*.

And undoubtedly Roger Fry's weekly lectures on Italian art, with lantern slides, were of the greatest significance to Carrington during her Slade years. Fry had already found a forum through his essay writing on art for the *Athenaeum* and *Burlington* magazines. And, as the subjects he wrote about suggest, a lecture by Fry was just as likely to include a reference to the art of the bushmen or his theories of aesthetic emotion, as the early Italians.

Fry's focus and originality were so far reaching they not only altered the face of his time but seeped into the next. Fry's gifts as an interpreter guaranteed him a captive audience, and his lectures helped create the mood of the moment among students for the Italians: for Sassetta, a Sienese; for the simplicity of form of, Giotto and Fra Angelico, both Florentines; for the colour of the Venetians, Titian and Tintoretto; for the fantastic world of the Roman Piero di Cosimo; and for the Umbrian, Piero della Francesca whose spacial

the nervous impetuosity of line or the light of Carrington's personal vision in her later drawings. And although Augustus John's legendary prowess as a draughtsman had made drawing a wholly desirable artform in itself, the fold through the middle of *Bedford Market* suggests it was stuffed into a portfolio or drawer and forgotten. Carrington never agreed with Ingres that drawing was the

clarity gave his work a serenity and timelessness.

And in the term that Carrington came to the Slade, Fry mounted an exhibition of the art of 'Manet and the Post-Impressionists', so coining a term for modern French art from the previous three decades. It is now hard to appreciate the very real horror experienced by the audiences who flocked to see this exhibition at the New Grafton Galleries. For a while Fry became the Aunt Sally of the art establishment; Harold Gilman was moved to make a new commandment: 'thou shalt not put a blue line around thy mother'; Walter Sickert led the older generation in denouncing Fry's teachings as 'pernicious nonsense'; even Brown, Tonks and Steer exerted every influence they could to dissuade Slade students from visiting the exhibition and catching the virus of the new art.

But the tide had turned; while Sickert continued to wear his high collars up, Fry turned his down and for Carrington's generation Fry was 'the high priest of art of the day, and could and did make artistic reputations overnight. To be noticed … was an undoubted honour.'[11] No artist remained unaffected or could ever be the same again. In Gertler's words: 'The entry of Cézanne, Gaugin, Matisse etc., upon my horizon was equivalent to the impact of the scientists of this age upon a simple student of Sir Isaac Newton.'[12]

Artistically, the years leading up to World War I were a time of great intercourse between groups and nations, and in many ways this exhibition – there was another in 1912 which included the British – highlighted the burgeoning modern movement. New exhibiting bodies, born out of opposition to the ageing NEAC, began to show the work of the Cubists, Futurists, Impressionists, Neo-Realists and Primitives.

In spite of her youth, Carrington was already a discriminating artist and although bombarded by the wealth of new artistic ideas from the Continent, she still managed to retain a place for the sensibilities of English art, which also spoke to her condition. In this she had her allies. Nevinson was four years older than Carrington and already a senior student at the Slade when she arrived. His encouraging advice to her in 1912, albeit a little patronizing, was sound: 'I am convinced there is

something in you if only you can find your right track and others do not send you off into wrong ones & now that Art is in this Anarchic & egoistical condition with absolutely no two standards of taste alike in a little time you will probably find yourself hopelessly lost, I know Gertler & I are always getting muddled … & above all don't get into this post-impressionistic cleverness of pretending to be a great[er] fool than you are & paint your own time & the life about you.'[13]

Of the Post-Impressionists Cézanne was Carrington's particular star. Through years of experimentation Cézanne had attained a simple expression of feeling through simplified forms, where mass replaced detail and creation was the aim not imitation. Fry called it 'Significant Form', and Clive Bell later expounded on it in 1914 in his book, *Art*. Carrington and Gertler bought postcards of Cézanne's work from the British Museum shop, and examined them in every detail so as to understand their rare beauty and freedom from technicality. Through copying came the discovery of how an effect had been achieved and Carrington never lost the habit; even in the late 1920s she was still painting 'Giottos', the artist she most often came back to.

And so as Carrington added to her firmament of stars she became a confirmed eclectic, drawing her inspiration across countries, centuries and divides. But of her near contemporaries at home, Augustus John and Aubrey Beardsley held sway. Carrington's pen and wash drawing, *Woman in a Chemise*, is so convincingly John-like it could quite easily be one of his drawings of gypsy tribes and is clearly Carrington learning by emulation. Carrington's pencil drawing, *Reclining Nude*, c.1915, faintly highlighted with sanguine, must almost certainly be the one that Gertler referred to when he wrote: 'That little German girl you drew nude, dances *excellently*. She has a lovely little figure to clasp.'[14] It is a lovely example of Carrington's clear, directly stated line and gives some hint of her nudes to come. The paring of superfluous lines also suggests that she may have been looking at the work of the Greek vase painters; Beardsley, whom Roger Fry called the 'Fra Angelico of Satanism', and the visionary poet-painter William Blake. Barbara's harlequin costume for a *Souvenir of a Slade Dance*

Woman in a Chemise, c.1915, pen, ink and wash on paper. Private collection

Reclining Nude, c. 1915,
pencil and sanguine on
paper, 28 × 44.5
(11 × 17½). Courtesy:
Anthony d'Offay Gallery,
London

could have been directly lifted from Beardsley's illustrations for the *Scarlet Pastorale* for the London Year Book.

But among her peers, the most formative and important artistic relationship Carrington had was with Gertler. Gertler's patron Edward Marsh described his protégé to Rupert Brooke: 'his mind is deep and simple and I think he's got the feu sacré.'[15] Marsh also considered Gertler 'the greatest genius of the age'.[16]

For twelve volatile years Gertler was Carrington's intimate friend. They visited museums together, swopped books and reproductions of paintings and they read the same writers: the works of Donne, Dostoevsky and Nietzche. Gertler wrote to Carrington: 'I too am proud to be *your* friend, because there are very few people in the world for whom I have a respect as great as I have for you! To be in your beautiful presence is to feel uplifted and stimulated the whole time. Whenever I am with you I feel the same as I do in front of a real work of art, or as one feels at a moment of some emotional or religious conception.'[17]

Carrington and Gertler's reputations went before them, and when Nina Hamnett invited them to tea she felt as if she was inviting a god and goddess. It was 1911, Carrington arrived hatless, wearing one red shoe and one blue, and Nina preserved Gertler's teacup unwashed on the mantelpiece for a month after.

But in loving Gertler there was an innate menace to Carrington's freedom and it was the first of the troublesome relationships she had, for which she is so unfairly castigated. Gertler fell in love with an artist but what he wanted was a wife, and he wrote to Carrington: 'You certainly ought to learn something about cooking. I should always prefer my girl friends to be better cooks than artists.'[18]

Gertler needed always to have Carrington in his sights or in his mind and through trying to possess her so completely he might as well have tried to bottle the wind. After an unsuccessful week together at Cholesbury, when the inequality of their desires came to a head, Carrington wrote honestly to Gertler: 'Yes, it is my work that comes between us, but I cannot put that out of my life because it is too much myself now. If I had not my love for painting I should be a different person ... I at any rate could not work at all if I lived with you every day.'[19]

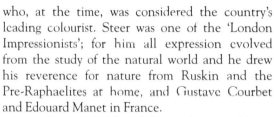

At the age of eighteen Carrington's own sexuality had not awakened. She had been brought up to stifle sensual feelings and what she sought in friendship was the platonic ideal of love between soul and soul. Carrington and Gertler were matched in their passion for their art but not in their sexual appetite for each other, and the agonies of their situation have been preserved through their letters. For Gertler, friendship alone was a poor form of happiness and, even though she felt 'more improved by him than anyone' when they talked about painting, Carrington was indifferent to marriage.[20]

In 1912, by the end of her second year, Carrington had notched up sufficient notice, credits and prizes to be made (with William Roberts) the much coveted Slade scholar for the next two years, with a scholarship of £35 per annum.[21] It was an important achievement because it meant she could continue at the Slade. In that same year she won the Melville Nettleship Prize for Figure Composition and second prize for Figure Painting. In 1913 she would win first prize for Figure Painting and first prize for Painting from the Cast.

Painting at the Slade was supervised by Steer who, at the time, was considered the country's leading colourist. Steer was one of the 'London Impressionists'; for him all expression evolved from the study of the natural world and he drew his reverence for nature from Ruskin and the Pre-Raphaelites at home, and Gustave Courbet and Edouard Manet in France.

As we have seen, the Slade teachers would not assimilate the ideas of Post-Impressionism into their teaching, and for the time being Carrington's figure paintings were by tone, in the manner of Velasquez. Apart from the Antique Room the Slade had a model in every room and its pedagogical principles were Life Room based. Poses were held for a fortnight and the prizewinner had the privilege of setting the pose and selecting her place for her easel.

Carrington's prize-winning painting in 1912, of a reclining nude placed against a dark background, was a fine academic painting in the tradition of the old masters. The muscles of the twisted and foreshortened right arm are beautifully rendered and the generally brown palette only goes up a notch in the rouge of the model's cheeks and the ginger of her pubic hair.

ABOVE LEFT *Carrington*, Mark Gertler, 1912, gouache on paper, 47.5 × 38.75 (18¾ × 15¼). Edgar Astaire Collection

ABOVE Carrington and Mark Gertler, c. 1911. Luke Gertler

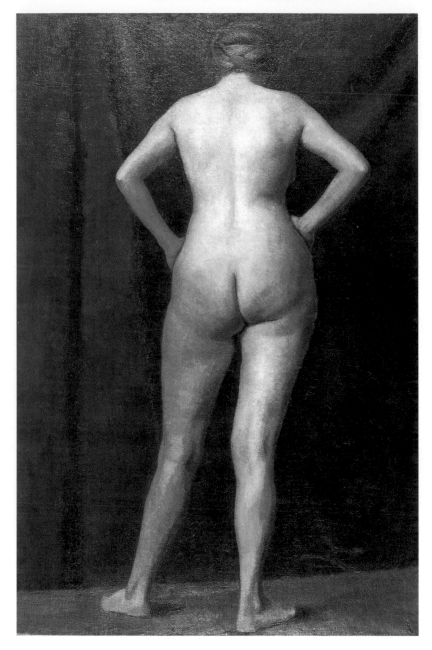

Standing Nude, 1913, oil on canvas, awarded Slade first prize for Figure Painting. College Art Collections, University College London

In the winter term of 1912, as a change from the usual curriculum, Mrs Sargant-Florence returned to the school, where she had been a student under Alphonse Legros in the 1880s, to give lectures and demonstrations on her new-found passion: fresco and tempera painting. The following summer, Carrington, with her friend Constance Lane, completed a splendid cycle of three larger than life-size frescoes for the provident Lord Brownlow, on the library wall of Brownlow Hall in a block adjacent to his nineteenth-century gothic palace of Ashridge in the Chilterns.

Finding a patron, thanks to Constance, prepared to take the risk with such an untried art form in Britain, was fortunate indeed. The more usual method of mural decoration in the notoriously damp British climate had been to paint on canvas in a studio, with prepared oil colours in opaque tones, and then to transfer the work to the intended wall. Painting fresco meant working in situ with wet plaster and the transparent tones of watercolours using natural pigment. It was a challenging and arduous job since the painting of an area of fresh plaster had to be finished before it hardened (i.e. within six to eight hours) and meant making a long day of it, with little room for error. It was also a messy one with everyone involved looking like 'a whitewashed sepulcure'.[23]

By way of preparation Carrington had begun to work in tempera on gesso at Bedford and corrections to her fresco were made in tempera on dry plaster. She had seen 'some most amazingly good old frescoes, about 1100–1200 AD';[24] had begun to imagine Giotto nativities in every view and, most importantly of all, had visited an exhibition of the Pre-Raphaelites, where she saw Holman Hunt's *The Hireling Shepherd* and thought it amazing.

The girls stayed with Constance's mother in a cottage two miles away at Nettleden, and Carrington was in her element, writing to John Nash, her new-found friend, painterly letters, full of observations and ideas for pictures which were bubbling up like her pot of parchment size. At a time when elms 'showing their ankels' were a feature of the English landscape, local bucolic scenes of hoeing, sheep shearing and the hay harvest were chosen for the frescoes.[25] Of the three, Carrington certainly painted *Hoeing* (see p. 49), and there are

A year on, in the *Standing Nude*, Carrington's treatment of the woman's strongly lit figure using pearlescent, oystershell colours for the body tones, and blue highlights for the crevices and hollows of her back and buttocks, showed her confident and skilful use of colour and provoked Gertler's admiration: 'I *loved* that nude painting of yours. What a good painter you are!'[22]

also signs of her collaboration on the other two panels. Constance was a perfect companion and she sang while they worked, 'lustily with much force old ballades & folk songs & Handel'.[26]

Carrington wrote to Nash: 'Since Monday I have been here, oh but it is a most wonderful country! You, & Paul should just see the trees, & green fields like lettuces, you could almost eat them they are so luscious … it is altogether a very happy place. We go up each day to Ashridge, (an ancestoral seat, with a most amazing early Italian garden & trees) to do our frescoe. I am drawing the big cartoon hard. 6 ft by 5 ft. It *is* a job. But so exciting. I spend the mornings in fields drawing big heavy elms for it & small village boys come, & pose in the garden in the evening. Today the mason gave me a lesson in plastering, it is good to do. Mixing matter, & sand, then slaping it on the wall with "floats" & making it as smooth as marble. About 6 workman are running about erecting scaffolding, & carrying buckets. Lane and me feel like great masters controlling this band of men & having the big wall to cover with our works of art. Frescoe painting is awfully hard all this afternoon I have been struggling to learn.'[27]

Clearly Carrington's technique was sound because when she took Ralph Partridge to see the frescoes twelve years later she wrote to Gerald Brenan: 'They are still intact, and haven't fallen down or changed colour which just proves that frescoes can last in England, which everyone always denies.'[28]

Carrington's detailed subject of hoeing, in a well ordered land, had all the elements of the things that she took joy in at the time. Each panel was unified with a border of burnt gold and cerulean blue, and Carrington's use of colours and forms to create vistas was expert. The meticulously painted companionable planting of larkspur, cabbages, sunflowers and onions in serried ranks creates a foreground. The dusty pink of the woman's simple dress takes us one step back without separating us from the flowering sedum and the silk back of the bewhiskered man's waistcoat, which have the same colour. The larkspur's blue appears again in the wuthering elms and highlights the cabbage leaves. Golden corn lights up the middle and far distance, glows again in the sunflowers, the young boy's breeches and the wooden handles of the hoes. Rape yellow for the field behind draws our eye even further and so the distance continues to recede around pockets of woods and fields bounded by hedgerows.

After the success of the Ashridge frescoes, several projects were discussed. The father of another Slade girl, Marjorie Debenham, had the commission to renovate three small villages and build a village hall at Tonerspuddle, near Dorchester. Unfortunately, the proposal for a decoration 11' by 30' never came off. Neither did the scheme Carrington embarked on with John and Paul Nash for a church near Uxbridge. Carrington had chosen the subject of Jacob meeting Rebecca but the Bishop's permission was slow in coming and then impending war put a stop to negotiations.

But also the prospect of collaboration had made Carrington anxious. She needed some cajoling to send her designs to John Nash whereas there had been no such self censor when working on her own project and he wrote to her: 'Do not make yourself unhappy over your design & I hope you will not infect me also with the feeling that one's work is not good enough.'[29] John and Paul were beginning to exhibit their work and tried to persuade Carrington to join them, but she would not and these are the first inklings of Carrington's exacting spirit, threaded through with the diffidence that did her such a disservice.[30]

24

Hurstbourne Tarrant 1914–1917
2 Own Voice

Slade students at this time were freebooters and chameleon in their colours; by turn vagabond, harlequin and scholar. Despite the fact that moving house 'meant pantechnicons drawn across country by a traction engine', Carrington's family had 'migrated at regular intervals' during her childhood and she had formed no real association with any one place.[1] But she was looking for the place that she could call home; her country. And so, for the time being Carrington's life was nomadic and clearly infected with the roving spirit she found in the poetry and prose of the 'super tramp' W. H. Davies, and the gypsy way of life that the Romany rye Augustus John had introduced her to.

Inevitably the transition from being a student and an 'apprentice', to graduating and becoming an 'artist', was fraught with difficulties, not least because Carrington was bound to her family financially and all the constraints that that imposed. Nonetheless, Carrington made titanic efforts to retain her hard-won independence, struggling to find ways of earning sufficient money to pay for her lodgings in the 'pickle Jammy gloom' of Soho, and her Chelsea studio.[2]

It was a penurious time. Carrington later wrote: 'I think the lack of money is perhaps more sordidly grim than anything. I've known it in London, walking from Waterloo to Hampstead because I hadn't a penny. Eating twopenny soup packets, meal after meal, in a smelling studio in Brompton Rd.'[3]

Even the most successful of Carrington's contemporaries found living by their painting alone virtually impossible. Gertler was the most serious singleminded artist there was and, for a time was assured a small monthly subsidy from Edward Marsh, yet he had to borrow money and ultimately turn to teaching to survive. The options open to

an artist were: to exhibit and hope to sell, which would necessitate being maintained while working towards that end; to enter competitions for prize money; to work to commission and risk the compromises that that entailed; or to teach.

Carrington exhibited her work in group exhibitions more often than is generally thought, but her reluctance to align herself with any one group also meant a disinclination to exhibit and she did so relatively rarely. In addition, it was a world in which men defined the terms of work and value. The prevalent attitude towards 'woman's art' was expressed in the radical magazine *Colour* which reported in 1915 that the paintings of a woman showing at the Fine Art Galleries did 'not suggest the prettiness rather general in woman's art, but contain real virility'.[4]

Carrington sold her first drawing for £5 8s through an exhibition of the New English Art Club in 1914 and was overjoyed because it was enough to pay Percy Young's bill for materials she had had on credit. Gertler felt that it proved she could, before long, be earning her living at her work. But at the same time Carrington was highly critical of the NEAC style of 'nicely matched mauves & greens … like a drapers shop "soft" coloured materials', and she did not think much more of the 'dull' pictures exhibited at the London Group.[5]

Carrington appeared to have no sense of posterity; she gave up the Slade habit of signing and dating her work as soon as she left the school. The present, living life to the lees and improving as a painter, by painting regularly, were all she seemed to care about. She also had innate dignity and was much affected by what she felt to be ugly or vulgar; exhibiting, which was like casting pearls before swine, fell into this category. Gertler gauged Carrington's feelings absolutely as she revealed in

OPPOSITE *Uplands around Hurstbourne Tarrant,* c.1916, oil on canvas, 62 × 51.2 (24¼ × 20⅛). Courtesy: Anthony d'Offay Gallery, London

replying to a letter of his: 'When you said that the artist's name didn't matter in a picture and you did not want to be a big artist yourself, only a creator, I felt I loved you more than I ever have before.'[6]

An indication that Carrington entered competitions for prize money appears in Rutherston's letter-drawing to Carrington. Captioned 'Oh that horible "Prix de Rome"' Rutherston pictured Carrington at her easel in painter's smock with palette and brush, surrounded by symbols of the countryside; a log and hatchet, a cockerel, a lamb, and a tin of green paint all point to the subject that Carrington was painting for her entry. The Rome Scholarship was worth £200 but it also meant spending three years in Rome and Carrington would not have been happy spending so long away from England.

As early as 1912, when in her second year at the Slade, Carrington had painted pictures as commissions, from postcards, and taken pupils. A share in a house could be found for £9 a year, a studio in Chelsea cost about 10s a week and Carrington could charge 5s for a painting lesson. Her determination to be independent was such that she even considered accepting a job as teacher of drawing at St Helen's High School, Abingdon. But Carrington was temperamentally unsuited to any fixed post and it would have been the death knell to her ambitions as a painter.

What Carrington needed was the stimulation of London where she could spend her mornings at the London Library; forenoons to early evening in her studio (maybe tea with Augustus John in one of the Belgian cafés in Fitzrovia); perhaps a Bach sonata played by Madame Suggia at the Aeolian Hall or *The Magic Flute* watched from Lord Esher's box at the Royal Opera House; followed by a late

Letter drawing,
5 June c. 1917

supper at Kettner's or an Armenian café where they played dominoes late into the night. And she found a good ruse for keeping up this way of life when she took on pupils, at one time teaching the children of Willoughby de Brook; Alaric, the son of the Belgian Baron de Forest and 'that little brute of a Joan Laking'[7]. Until, that is, war came.

Few people were prepared for it. Certainly most of the artists 'had only the haziest ideas as to what was going on in the rest of Europe'.[8] With war, London was horribly changed and the gaiety gone. The streets became peopled with amputees returning from the Front and the jaundiced aspect of munition workers, their faces stained yellow with TNT. And in the once peaceful parks, office-pale young men, erstwhile clerks now in khaki, did bayonet practice with horrible yells on straw-sacking effigies of the Kaiser.

Night became a hell-time, the beauty of the once black sky illuminated like Blackpool with strobing searchlights, and the silence torn to pieces with the crashing and banging of heavy artillery which shattered Carrington's nerves. By day, city life, with the 'Foul yellow fogs & rain'[9] and the 'square shapes of London houses and square slits of sky' made London detestable.[10]

In 1914 Carrington's parents struck camp once again and moved from Bedford to Ibthorpe House in the Hampshire village of Hurstbourne Tarrant, also known as Uphusband. Carrington had been oscillating between the stimulation of London, and the intellectual poverty of existence with her family for some while. She found that: 'Everything they say jars so terribly. They are so commonplace and material. This morning I just longed to run away from them all, and escape to London. You can never know what it is to have a Mother and family, and surroundings like those people in "the Way of all Flesh". Like "Ann Veronica's" parents.'[11]

Hampshire was a country of deep, long valleys and chains of lofty hills and heathland. Fast flowing streams spliced through narrow fields and winding single-track roads gave out onto meadows and copses of the vale. And in Hampshire Carrington found a country that she loved better than any other, with a rich vein to plunder for painting. There are endless descriptions in

Carrington's letters of painting neighbouring gardens and big, cumbersome landscapes of the hump-backed, beech be-clumped downs topped by gibbets; grim reminders of Cobbett's day. And so the beauty of the country and 'adventures in barns with cow-herders cutting mangles by candlelight' offered some compensations.[12]

Ibthorpe House was an imposing square-built Georgian farmhouse surrounded by outbuildings, one of which Carrington made into a studio. Her bedroom was at the top of the house and Carrington described to Christine Kühlenthal how she

decorated it: 'I painted the cupboard a lovely blue & red & green, & the board round the bottom of the wall, (scurtain board?) green, & the window sill & my bed bright blue. & distempered all the walls a creamy white.'[13] And it was from the lofty height of this room that Carrington drew the 'big round spotted field like a basin covered with dark irregular bushes' of scrubby hawthorn and juniper, that loomed up in front of her.[14]

In an exquisite evocation of the character of a place, Carrington's large watercolour painting of the *Hill in Snow at Hurstbourne Tarrant* shows her

Hill in Snow at Hurstbourne Tarrant, 1916, watercolour on paper, 53.9 × 64.1 (21¼ × 25¼). Private collection

27

fascination for the abstract forms of landscape and is the first of the intimate and graceful place portraits that we have come to identify with Carrington. She wrote to Gertler: 'Today it is snowing white, and a piercing wind. But I love the hugeness of it. The great space between one and the hills opposite.'[15]

Carrington admired the snowscapes and naturalism of Pieter Bruegel and looked at *The Hunters in the Snow* when she visited the Kunsthistorisches Museum in Vienna in 1922. Carrington's own snowscape was painted six years earlier and had, by contrast, the tranquility and snow-muffled power of a relatively wild and unpopulated landscape. The hill is set against the pale-resulting sky that comes after the blanket snowfall which so radically changes the aspect of a place. The boles of the trees, sodden and darkened with wet, are thrown into relief against the brightness of the snow and limpid sky, and draw our eye in a different way from usual, up and beyond.

Carrington's preoccupation with the great mass and domination of land, topped by very little sky, and with rhythm, in the globe-like hill which looks as if it might bowl itself out of the picture, became an exaggerated feature of her landscapes.

In a second painting of the uplands around Uphusband, Carrington made a lyrical study in brilliant greens of well-watered meadows divided up by hedgerows. One field in particular draws the eye, because it is diamond shaped, and above it scuds a single clumping cloud in an otherwise blameless blue sky. And, as will be seen, this painting is slightly unusual in that it is an upright landscape, which allows for a huge and uncharacteristic amount of sky.

Carrington was a naturalist in her work; not in the sense that it was photorealistic but in that she conveyed what she saw in a recognizable form. As has been seen, Carrington had Holman Hunt's *The Hireling Shepherd* in mind when she was painting her fresco. This affinity with the Pre-Raphaelites was most apparent in the preliminary stage when Carrington drew the countryside almost topographically, accurately rendering the outlines of hills, and carefully defining detail with calligraphic squiggles. The simplification of forms, which she generally aimed for, came with painting. Because

of this, Carrington's drawings and watercolours of landscape, both of which were only ever preparations for painting, often have a quite different sensibility to the finished oil.

Carrington's work was inherently autobiographical, portraying as she did the people and the places that populated her world. Later, in her glass paintings and decorative painting the element of fantasy that occupied her private moments would creep in, but for the time being she painted what everyone could see.

Carrington had a critical eye and captured faces with the 'preternatural acuteness of her vision of others'.[16] Consequently, she did not always make portraits that were comfortable and a disparity appears in the ways that she treated her subjects according to how she perceived them and the place they held in her affections.

Carrington's portrait of *The Boot Boy* in his workaday weeds was probably painted in Bedford before 1914 and is her earliest surviving portrait. The picture is of a hamster-cheeked young man in the flush of youth, for which Carrington chose the simple device that Titian used of placing the sitter in front of a single colour that projects him forwards, and the picture is so fluidly painted it might be on an oak panel for all the evidence there is of the texture of canvas.[17]

Carrington was a favourite with her father and he with her. Although she knew little of his past life, she learnt of the regard in which he had been held, 'by sahibs and natives alike', when his Anglo-Indian cronies came with tales of his kindnesses.[18] Carrington wrote to Gertler after Samuel's death in 1918: 'I loved my father for his rough big character. His rustic simplicity and the great way he lived inside himself and never altered his life to please the conventions, or people of this century. He would have been exactly the same if he had lived under Elizabeth.'[19] And she loved to draw and paint 'that cragged hoary old man with his bright eyes, and huge helpless body'.[20]

Swopping from the sixteenth-century device she had used for the boot boy to the less formal style that Cézanne used in the portrait of his father *Louis-Auguste Cézanne reading l'Evénement*, 1866, Carrington painted Samuel in 1915, in a cretonne-covered chair, with the pathos of the tail end of a life, and in so doing introduced the element of psychology which gave the edge to her portraits.

Both *The Boot Boy* and *Samuel Carrington* were building blocks for what has come to be Carrington's most famous portrait, that of Lytton Strachey, whom she met in 1915.

In June 1923 Carrington recalled: 'I myself could not stand the few years of loneliness and isolation that I lived through after I left the Slade.'[21] Identity, according to R.D.Laing, requires the existence of another by whom one is known and Carrington met that someone in Giles Lytton Strachey. Carrington's passion for Lytton would have the same influence upon the rest of her life as the waxing and waning of the moon has upon the tides.

Sacheverell Sitwell described the common astonishment of their friends: 'There was certainly an aura attaching to her, too, and one cannot but have every sympathy with the painter Mark Gertler, who loved her perhaps even at this time, and could not understand her devotion to the freakish and anything but kind-tongued Lytton Strachey … In her distinctive yet classless appearance she epitomised those few months and years of her own youth.'[22]

Against all odds, Carrington and Lytton formed a platonic allegiance which weathered all sorts of complications and became a 'marriage' for life. Lytton was thirty-five and valetudinarian; Cambridge educated and one of the group of friends that came to be known as Old Bloomsbury. He was a writer, but yet to be published, and his friends considered him the most brilliant of them all. He was also homosexual.

Carrington was twenty-two, in rude health and the appearance of being a constant nymph. But in Lytton Carrington found a light of mind that she could revere and, most importantly, she wrote many years later when looking back: 'He was, and this is why he was everything to me, the only person to whom I never needed to lie, because he never expected me to be anything different to what I was.'[23]

In a photograph album Carrington made for Lytton, with vellum spine and printed paper boards, she pasted in a print of an eighteenth-

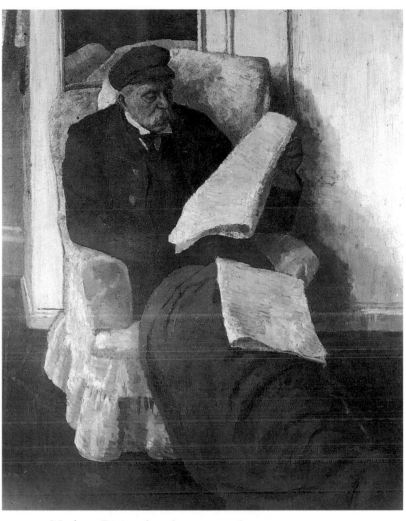

Samuel Carrington, 1915, oil on canvas, 40.6 × 35.6 (16 × 14). Private collection

century Moslem Divine kneeling on cushions, clasping a book in one hand and stroking his beard with the other. The figure bore a remarkable resemblance to the equally yogi-like Lytton. Carrington had crossed out Moslem replacing it with English and adding 'L.S. twentieth century'. It was how she always saw him.

Carrington explained Lytton's attraction for her to Gerald Brenan: 'Sometimes with Lytton I have amazing conversations. I mean not to do with this world, but about attitudes and states of mind, and the purpose of living. That is what I care for most in him. In the evenings suddenly one soars without corporeal bodies on these planes of thought.'[24] But it was also for the humour they shared; Lytton was very funny, as his letter to Carrington from

Letter drawing, January 1919

Tidmarsh Mill in 1918 shows: '[t]he beans frighten me. I was told to pick some of them, but they frighten me. As for the raspberries, I feel as if I should never worm my way under the nets. La Legg confesses herself baffled by the hens – after pretending last night that she could catch them without the slightest difficulty. I am in favour of making them tipsy – it seems to me, short of shooting them, the only plan.'[25]

Carrington met Lytton at Asheham House, the country home of Virginia and Leonard Woolf. It was in the Ouse Valley underneath the Sussex Downs and was 'a place of great strangeness and beauty'.[26] Carrington had been invited to join the

Letter drawing, 4 February 1917

party of Clive Bell, Duncan Grant, Mary Hutchinson and Lytton, and could not think why. She had taken a walk across the Downs with Lytton when, attracted by her androgynous appearance, he embraced her. Outraged that 'that horrid old man with a beard kissed me!' Carrington plotted to steal into his bedroom as he slept and to revenge herself upon the offending brittle beard.[27] The legend has it that Lytton woke and beguiled Carrington with his eyes; it was the beginning of a mutual fascination.

They discussed physical relations, even gave them a try, but 'the management of spectacles and pince-nez while making love' (Marjorie Strachey intended writing a pamphlet on the subject) was only one of the hindrances, as Lytton explained in a letter in August 1916 to John Maynard Keynes:

> When I'm winding up the toy
> of a pretty little boy,
> – Thank you, I can manage pretty well;
> But how to set about
> To make a pussy pout
> – *That* is more than I can tell.[28]

Sex was not going to work between them, and in a letter to Lytton in 1917 Carrington jokingly described how: 'Hours were spent in front of the glass last night strapping the locks back, and trying to persuade myself that two cheeks like turnips on the top of a hoe bore some resemblance to a very well nourished youth of sixteen.'[29] Carrington was petite, several heads shorter than Lytton and had a quirky way of dressing. Lytton was bohemian looking and emaciated. Both together and apart they were stared at in the street. Carrington's hair attracted hostile yells and Lytton's unfashionable beard provoked 'goat' bleatings.

They were undoubtedly a curious looking couple but the point was, and is, there are 'a great deal of a great many kinds of love' and Carrington and Lytton found a kind that suited them.[30] They were both image breakers and advancing spirits who, each in their way, helped fashion the age in which they lived.

Quite bluntly, their friends were appalled. They thought the match ill-conceived and Virginia would later joke to her sister Vanessa of an evening at Tidmarsh Mill when Carrington and Lytton quietly withdrew, 'ostensibly to copulate' but were found to be reading aloud from Macaulay.[31] And if Lytton did Carrington a disservice at all, it was not by not loving her sufficiently but by failing to have the courage at that time to acknowledge to his oldest friends how important she was to him.

These friends, most of whom had known each other from university days at Cambridge, became known as the Bloomsbury Group, or Bloomsberries, as Molly MacCarthy nicknamed them. They continued to meet in Thoby Stephen's house in Gordon Square and came to include Thoby's sisters, Vanessa and Virginia.

Many years later, in her diary, Carrington puzzled over the 'quintessence' of Bloomsbury and concluded: 'It was a marvellous combination of the Highest intelligence, & appreciation of Literature combined with a lean humour & tremendous affection. They gave it back wards and forwards to each other like shuttlecocks only the shuttlecocks multiplied as they flew in the air.'[32] But on the whole they were Lytton's friends and Carrington's role in Bloomsbury was a satellite one. Carrington's friends did not form cliques in the way that

aviron

Bloomsbury did and her cronies came from the Slade; they chose to live around the Hampshire-Wiltshire borders and had their studios in Chelsea, whereas the Bloomsbury Group lived in Sussex and Bloomsbury.

Carrington began the portrait of Lytton in the winter of 1916. When painted, Lytton's inelegan-

Letter drawing, 10 August 1917

Carrington and Lytton reading Gibbon c. 1916

Lytton on the beach near
Tal-y-Cafn, N. Wales, 1916

Letter drawing, March/
April 1929

cies somehow became assets. With his ridiculously crane-like limbs, which occupied no more space than a bedpan in the bed, and his natural inclination to keep still for long periods at a time, he was a gift to an artist.

There never has been much market in other people's ancestors and the power of a successful portrait comes from the fascination it creates for the sitter. With her portrait of Lytton, Carrington established her voice as uniquely, identifiably her own. It took about two months and all the while she was brimming with confidence because she knew she had pulled it off, writing in her diary on 1 January 1917 when she had finished: 'I wonder what you will think of it when you see it. I sit here, almost every night it sometimes seems, looking at your picture, now tonight it looks wonderfully good, and I am happy. But then I dread showing it. I should like to go on always painting you every week, wasting the afternoon loitering, and never, never showing you what I paint. It's marvellous having it all to oneself. No agony of the soul. Is it vanity? No because I don't care for what they say. I hate only the indecency of showing them what I have loved.'

Every inch of this sage-like portrait is touched with loving attention and manages to penetrate the bodily camouflage with which Lytton attempted to conceal himself. The scale of colours Carrington used perfectly expressed the emotional range she sought. The warm squirrel reds of Lytton's horn-rimmed spectacles and brillo-pad beard, the marbled pages of his ubiquitous book, and the paisley shawl, contrast with the coolness of the blues of the pillow and background and create volume and depth.

Even at the age of thirty-six there was something milk-puddingish about Lytton; he was the sort of man who liked to be brought cups of Bovril. Come winter, come summer he dressed for the cold. And it is irresistible not to find an echo resounding between Carrington's portrait of her father in his old age, immobilized by the red rug which makes a caterpillar of his legs, Lytton's portrait, and her painting *Job's Comforters*, – made for a Slade Summer Competition – of poor, white bearded Job naked but for a long red cloth covering his loins, and humiliated by his so-called comforters who aggravate his distresses. The red rug in all three paintings, consciously or not, is symbolic of nurturing and with it transfers some of Carrington's affections.

At the beginning of the century there were several postal deliveries a day and a letter written by Carrington in the morning from the country could be expected to arrive in London in time to announce her arrival for tea. Regular periods apart from her friends, and an antipathy to the telephone, undammed a flood of letters, which

expressed 'the nakedness of a female's mind', and which make Carrington one of the great letter writers of her time.[33]

Carrington first came to light as a writer of vivid, painterly, illuminated letters when they were published in 1970. Virginia Woolf had a great relish for these letters written in purple ink 'tearing like a may-fly up and down the pages',[34] finding the writing her 'ideal in the way of hands'[35] and the letters themselves 'completely unlike anything else in the habitable globe.'[36]

Carrington wrote constantly to Noel while he served in the army in France, every week sending him papers and pamphlets and woodcuts she had made, and Noel felt that that giving side of her would never be fully known.

Carrington must have spent hours, almost daily, writing letters. To some extent they were a thief upon her painting time but they were also a way of focusing her ideas for pictures and calligraphic work, full of illustrations capturing the absurdities of her everyday life, for which we are the richer. Some of her illustrations anticipate the comic violence of Charlie Chaplin and Walt Disney's *Mickey Mouse*, which Carrington saw in 1930 and thought 'almost a work of genius!'[37] And Gerald Brenan would later say of Carrington's letters that they were like a 'gesture, speech, walk, expression, seen through a medium of words; ... Education has not deadened in you this mode of expression, has not, as it has for nearly all of us, reduced speech and writing to the level of a vulgar formula, through which we can barely let our own natures be recognised.'[38]

Carrington's life was almost entirely visual, and she wrote of everything she saw and felt in terms of colours and make-up. She was also a natural, runaway writer with her own personal lexicon of imagery. One of Carrington's correspondents, Rosamond Lehmann, took many aspects of Carrington's character for her painter/photographer heroine Anna Cory in *The Weather in the Streets*, saying of Anna's handwriting that it was: 'small, nervous, spidering, half formed, her style, child-like, vivid, ingenuously eccentric, her punctuation, a few capricious commas, made up an obscure yet revealing commentary on her character.'[39]

Carrington wrote as she spoke, always in a rush, with pen and ink – purple or green – or whatever came to hand; drunkenly; sometimes almost indecipherably because there were so many blots, or changes-of-mind strenuously obliterated with a barbed-wire spiralling. And, rather than go onto

TOP Letter drawing, 31 October 1918

ABOVE Letter drawing, August 1927

33

Letter drawing, 10 February 1917

a second page, she would crawl up the sides of her small notepaper and over the top again.

Her spelling was atrocious but her mispellings and coining of words were often peculiarly apt: 'Then a sogjourn – which I know is spelt wrong but I can't make it look better.'[40] And when she wrote: 'The yellow cat has passed away. Dead as a ducat' it suggests that she visualized the look of the words upon the page and imagined the colours of what she was saying.[41] Capital letters would punctuate the middle of sentences and sometimes the end of a word or line, and have the same halting effect as her gasp while speaking. But it was also an unintentionally Augustan way of giving quite ordinary words a sudden importance.

Carrington discovered that she had a gift for parodying another's style. When Carrington thought Clive Bell had unfairly criticized Bernard Shaw's play *Back to Methuselah* in the *New Republic*, she sent him a letter, ostensibly from Shaw. Bell was completely hoaxed and Carrington wrote to Lytton: 'I see a new aspect: a new avenue in life now! Forgery between lovers, enemies, dukes and

duchesses.'[42] She planned to write a send-up for Middleton Murry's new magazine: 'a little story about a charwoman and a lost hairpin in a drain. I promise you it will be accepted.'[43] And in July 1931 the *Week-End Review* announced Lytton's thumbnail sketches of six English historians, offering two guineas to whoever could write the best seventh sketch of the 'venerable' biographer himself in his own style; Carrington won. Carrington never felt the frustration with her writing that she felt with her painting because she had not chosen to be a writer, and so she set less store by it, never doubting that her stories would be accepted.

In this era people had a passion for documenting their times, and Carrington filled several albums with photographs using ready-made books with soft, green covers the colour of old files, and thin, brown leaves like the unrolled tobacco of cigars. Like letter writing, photographs captured everything that Carrington did – trips, latest paintings, parties – and not just for pasting into albums, but for exchanging with friends.

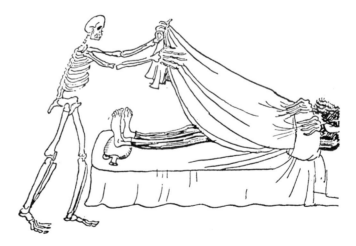

3 The Modern Movement. Black and White

'I didn't raise my boy to be a soldier. I brought him up to be my pride and joy' was a popular music-hall song that also reflected popular opinion. Most of Carrington's friends were conscientious objectors, fighting for the right not to fight, and needed to find other ways of contributing towards the war effort. Agricultural work was one of the options and, prompted by the need to find placements in the country, Lady Ottoline Morrell left Bloomsbury, where she had held her salon-style gatherings, to set up home in Oxfordshire, attracting to her, pied-piper-like, a coterie of artists of whom Carrington, introduced by Gertler, was one.

Ottoline was a striking woman 'of Elizabethan extravagance' and in Garsington Manor she found a house of equal character. Shandygaff Hall, as Carrington called it, had originally been built for a monastic order and its ponds had been mentioned in the Doomsday Book. From the back of the house the Italianate garden of linking 'rooms' sloped down to open fields and unrestricted views of the magnificent primordial Wittenham Clumps.

At Garsington Ottoline combined the Beardsley qualities of bohemian *fin de siècle*, the opulence of the Renaissance popes, and the libertinism of her own age. The wainscotting was painted peacock blue and Italian pictures hung alongside drawings by Augustus John and Henry Lamb, watercolours by Charles Conder, paintings by Duncan Grant and Gertler and a dozen other of the young male artists who came to her house and to whom she often formed strong attachments.

Ottoline was quixotic, possessive and tempestuous by turn. Virginia Woolf thought her a Medusa, and as Carrington discovered, there was a price to pay for her friendship. Ottoline meddled in Carrington's affair with Gertler and tried to persuade her into bedding with him; for Carrington 'this attack on the virgins is like the worst Verdun

on-slaughter'.[1] Thereafter Ottoline plainly disliked her and Carrington wrote: 'I am out of favour now! *completely*! I do not know why – But her ladyship loves & fondels me no more!'[2] The volte-face was also due to a rivalry that Ottoline felt with Carrington over Lytton.

Garsington was the only place where Carrington and Lytton could be together, untroubled, for long periods of time, doing what they liked doing best, which Lytton described in a letter that he hoped would induce Carrington to spend the whole of July there in 1916: 'I would translate the whole of French literature for you, and give you lectures on the whole of English-Latin, Greek, Portuguese, and Low Dutch to follow.'[3] But they were also so involved with one another Ottoline felt herself and the rest of her company forsaken.

In the evenings, in scenes that D.H.Lawrence used for *Women in Love*, the friends performed plays, Katherine Mansfield sang songs and the Byronic Gertler was an inspirational dancer. And, as Aldous Huxley described: 'of nights I have been sleeping out on the roof in company with an artistic young woman in short hair and purple pyjamas ... spending most of the night in conversation or in singing folk-songs and rag-time to the stars ... while early in the morning we would be wakened by a gorgeous great peacock howling like a damned soul while he stalked about the tiles showing off his plumage to the sunrise.'[4] Huxley was kinder to Carrington in his portrayal of 'Lollipop Hall' in *Crome Yellow* than he had been to Ottoline, whom he pilloried. As the character Mary, he described her 'moon-like innocence ... whose expression was one of ingenuous and often puzzled earnestness' but got his own back at Carrington's chasteness on the roof by giving her the surname Bracegirdle.[5]

But by day they worked, coming together at meal

Carrington as a living
sculpture, Garsington
Manor, *c.* 1917

times. Carrington made several paintings at Garsington. One wet Saturday afternoon after lunch,
Ottoline cajoled Carrington, Barbara Hiles, John
Nash, Duncan Grant and David Garnett (who was
not a trained painter) into decorating the long
room at the top of the original monastic building.
Rural scenes were decided upon and, remarkably,
all but Duncan had finished by tea time. And as
Duncan was Ottoline's favourite, he was coerced
into completing his mural the next day. Reluctant
to paint, David finished it for him and Ottoline
was delighted. On a later visit David discovered
that only 'Duncan's' work had escaped white-
washing. 'Carrington, who had painted an extremely charming sketch, always regarded this
discrimination, in favour of what was largely my
work, as an outrage.'[6] And one can sympathize
with her making 'a Goyaesque portrait of our Lady
of mystery which gave me some pleasure. But as

I made her look like a pole-cat it had to be
suppressed from the public eye.'[7]

Another day, excited by children playing naked
in a meadow, thigh-high in yellow tulips, Carrington painted them onto a huge panel of an old door
that Ottoline gave her. Carrington's portrait of the
Canadian poet Frank Prewett, who was introduced
to Garsington by Siegfried Sassoon, is, however,
the only painting known to have survived.
'Toronto' had some Sioux Indian blood, was one of
Ottoline's favourites, and had become one of her
stable of young men until he disgraced himself by
stealing the cheese money and making a pass at
Ottoline's teenage daughter, Julian. Gertler wrote
he 'mooches about like a faded Hamlet'[8], but
Carrington was stirred by him, 'looking strangely
lovely on a great sienna horse', and painted him in
his jerkin.[9]

Very few still lifes from this period have been

traced, but Carrington's sketchbooks are full of them and we know from her letters to Gertler that this is what she was painting. In one letter she described a picture of five apples, shading from green to yellow, and two orange pumpkins on a dark reddish cloth. She continued to work from the figure too, painting Barbara Hiles nude in the garden at Eleanor, West Wittering, and a monkey puzzle tree, writing to Gertler that it was 'to be better than that one by Paul Nash you so liked'.[10] She also had a model posing for a picture of St John the Baptist, a subject she was unlikely to have chosen unless it was for a commission or proposal for an ecclesiastical decoration.

Carrington was always conceiving ideas for pictures and painting them. Virginia Woolf's comments help throw some light on what happened to these pictures afterwards and why. When Virginia bought a house in Lewes in 1919 she teased: 'One of the chief decorations is going to be a large showpiece by Carrington, found in an attic at Asheham; doesn't that make you blush all over – upset the tea – and scald the cat?'[11] and commented astutely in another letter: 'Its odd that painting should appeal to your modesty as personal chastity appealed to our mothers.[12]

Carrington had been painting before her Slade days; Noel's schoolfriend Denis, who was 'as lovely as a Norwegian sailor', sat for her and Charlotte used to show these paintings, with pride, at her 'second Thursday in the month' tea parties.[13] Very little of Carrington's early work has survived from the years leading up to and during the Slade. Because Carrington struggled to pay Percy Young's bill for materials, it was inevitable that she would re-use canvases rather than buy new ones. Very often it is only by the artist letting paintings go, either by exhibiting or selling, that pictures survive. That Carrington rarely did either has robbed posterity of much of her work, which is now known only through her letters.

Also, persuading a conservative public of 'Bird's Custard Islanders' to buy paintings by artists of significant form was an uphill struggle and if artists were to continue experimenting they needed both financial and moral support. Partly inspired by a visit to the mosaics of the fourth and fifth centuries in Ravenna, Italy, Roger Fry on his return

had galvanized interest in communal mural projects as employment for artists and as a way of stimulating the British public out of its aesthetic morass. Enlightened patrons, such as the Borough Polytechnic, London, paid for their walls to be decorated. It was as a natural extension to this idea that Fry conceived the notion of a studio workshop where artists could earn a small regular income, decorating household objects in the new style, which could then be bought direct by the public.

In 1913, when the lease became free on 33 Fitzroy Square, Bloomsbury, Fry invited Vanessa Bell and Duncan Grant to join him as directors and took on the lease at his own expense. They painted the front door red, when all around it were black, hung a large signboard bearing the painted symbol of the omega from the first floor, placed Post-Impressionist canvases by Bell and Grant in two niches on the second floor, and called it the Omega Workshops.

Fry took his example from the medieval Italian workshop system whereby patronage, communal art and the anonymity of the artist had enjoyed a symbiotic success. Most of the artists invited to join came from the Slade. They were each paid 30s a week from Fry's own pocket and, in order not to detract from their own time for painting, attended the studio no more than three half days a week.

The studio was on the first floor, with simple trestle tables and good big windows for light. Using whatever material came to hand, be it paint or fabric, artists took risks in their designing that they might not allow themselves in easel painting, and they discovered that ideas from easel painting could be abstracted for decoration. Designs broke all the rules, rarely repeated patterns and were characterized by the largeness of their execution. Not minding or pre-determining how a design might be applied meant that the same design could as well be used for tea trays as bedheads.

And, as joy-in-the-making was a principle aim, blanks were bought for painting on. For furniture they used Gimson ladder-back chairs or even second-hand bamboo and each idiosyncratically painted piece showed what Fry described as 'the nervous tremor of the creator's hand'. When the objects were finished they were sent down to

Title page of *Lucretius on Death*, 1917, woodcut

the home but unlike anything the home had ever seen.

Because it is not well documented, Carrington's part in the creative fervour of the Omega Workshops is generally underestimated. But she was one of the founder members of the Omega Club formed in the spring of 1917, and we know from her letters, and from her brother Noel who sometimes met her at the end of a morning stint, that she worked there, and that she needed the money. We also know that Fry thought well of Carrington's work and employed her in 1917 on the restoration of Mantegna's cartoons, *The Triumphs of Caesar*, at Hampton Court Palace, and would select her work for the 'Nameless' exhibition in 1921.

An important aspect of the workshop ethos, coupled with Fry's Quaker sensibilities, was that all artists should work anonymously and that an aesthetic unanimity would be strived for. For this reason it has been difficult to gauge Carrington's overall contribution. One gets the sense that the 100 or so designs, which now form the Fry bequest at the Courtauld Institute Galleries, were carefully sifted. Nothing was signed and some of the attributions which have been made cannot be definitive. Fry's insistence on anonymity would have appealed to Carrington, but it has also effectively obscured her work there.

Carrington cut the woodblocks for the third Omega book *Lucretius on Death*, the basic book of libertinism, which was published in October 1917, and she seems to have taken for inspiration the proportions of pre-Columbian architecture. Fry was so pleased with the result that he took the unprecedented step of placing a full-length page advertisement in the *Burlington Magazine* to announce its publication.

It is said that Carrington cut the title page and the first letter but that Fry must have designed them, even though there is no evidence in his published letters to suggest this. Fry clearly took a proprietorial interest in the making of the woodcut and Carrington submitted several versions to him, which is why, I think, Fry's actual input has been misinterpreted.

Carrington had already, and with acclaim, designed and cut the woodblocks for the very first

the ground-floor showroom to be sold. As one might expect, the first customers to the Omega were unconventional: H. G. Wells, Virginia Woolf, Diaghilev and Gertrude Stein. Fry had wanted to reach the masses but, as his stand at the Ideal Home Exhibition in 1913 proved, he had as much chance as elevating a lead balloon.

Perhaps those who had sufficient courage to knock on the red door which had been branded immoral by the press, were not likely to be too abashed by what they saw. But the riot of decoration confronting them on chairs, screens, marquetry cupboards and boxes, oversized cushions for sandbagging black velvet settees, ceiling-to-floor curtains, bolts of printed linens and batik, tea cups, tea trays and bedheads, vases and candlesticks, and plain celadon china, must have taken their breath away. Everything you could want for

publication of the Hogarth Press, published six months previously in April 1917, and it would seem most unlikely that she would not do the same here. Roald Kristian designed and cut the woodblocks for the first two Omega books, *Simpson's Choice* and *Men of Europe*, both in 1915.

In *Original Woodcuts by Various Artists*, 1918, Fry's work was concerned, as Kristian's had been, with the bold opposition of black and white rather than the three tones of black, grey and white that Carrington achieved through a network of finely graded lines. And in the cartouche of figures holding the omega symbol on the title page, Fry's omega is round whereas Carrington's is ovoid. Carrington's lettering is more elongated than anything else seen on Omega material and certainly seems to come from her alphabet since she used the same M in her bookplate of a swan for Montague Shearman (p. 71), and the H, O & E in her honey label for David Garnett.

The Omega Workshops also listed 'Dress' in its *Descriptive Illustrated Catalogue* (1914), and in March 1917 when Carrington designed the costumes of the John Beauty Chorus, for the Monster Matinée war benefit at the Chelsea Palace Theatre, she ordered them to be made through the workshops.

The pantomime was given in aid of the Lena Ashwell Concerts for the Troops and was a history of Chelsea with reviews about Rossetti, Whistler and others. Carrington was on one of the numerous committees and her costumes were for the grand finale in tribute to Augustus John, when the chorus sang the refrain of Harry Graham and H. Fraser-Simson's song 'Augustus John'.

> John! John!
> How he's got on!
> He owes it, he knows it, to me!
> Brass earrings I wear,
> And I don't do my hair,
> And my feet are as bare as can be;
> When I walk down the street,
> All the people I meet
> They stare at the things I have on!
> When Battersea-Parking
> You'll hear folks remarking:
> 'There goes an Augustus John!'[14]

Honey label design for David Garnett at Charleston, 1917

Barbara Hiles and Faith Henderson toiled day and night to finish the costumes and, although it is a pity she left out the colours, Beatrice, Lady Glenavy, who joined the chorus of thirty-seven women, described what they wore: 'little coloured coats and long skirts over bare feet, and ... funny little hats with high crowns or scarves tied round our heads.'[15] These sound very like the clothes Carrington had been making for herself inspired by the aesthetically simple dresses she saw, for example, in *The Three Virtues of the Franciscan Legend* by Sassetta. Carrington cut her dresses only slightly more elaborately than those, with full skirts falling from a natural waistline below a shirtwaister. This style of dressing was never a fad with Carrington; apart from a rising hemline her daytime look changed very little and she was always known for her odd print frocks.

The Omega Workshops was a magnificent aberration which weathered six years of increasing hostility with Fry at the helm. It had been a courageous enterprise but by 1919, exhausted and financially broken, Fry was compelled to close it down.

Undoubtedly, the Omega was the most stimulating group enterprise in Carrington's working life but she worked best alone and it would have come to a natural end anyway. In an undated letter written to Gertler from Gower Street, Carrington said she had just been to a lecture on twelfth-century French sculpture at the Slade and found it 'very exciting, & exhilirating after that most depressing show at the Omega!!!'[16] Complete abstraction, even for decoration, did not have enough humanity in it for Carrington, and Fry was likely to be dismissive of anything else.

Carrington's fascination with the art of print-

Garsington Manor *c.* 1919
(l to r): Michael
Llewellyn-Davies,
Carrington, Julian Morrell,
Ralph Partridge

making dates from this time. With woodcuts she could give her painting side a rest, and made many of them, particularly in the years leading up to 1920. She loved the white-line engraving of Thomas Bewick; she also had a copy of *The Physician's Visit*, a fifteenth-century woodcut by Bartholomaeus de Glanvilla. She would visit the British Museum with Arthur Waley, who was Assistant Keeper of Oriental Prints and Drawings, to look at Italian woodcuts and Chinese books, and in August 1917 she wrote to Noel serving in France: 'I should like an engraving of Molière if you see one, or Madame du Chatalet in particular, Voltaire's friend. Please.' He had already sent her: 'an exquisite engraving from Rouen … [of] F. M.

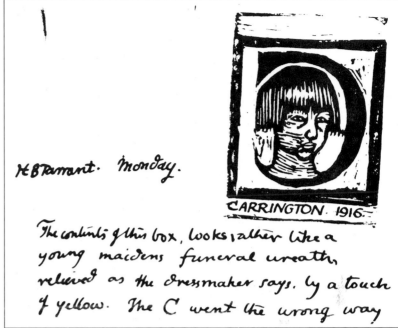

arouet de Voltaire – a very good print 1778', and these all informed her style.[17]

Carrington had already shown a facility for the interplay of light and dark in her drawing and had a good eye for the decorative planning of three tones. She used woodcuts to illustrate books, make bookplates and often just as something to slip into an envelope with her letters. They could be made almost anywhere and as Carrington was so often away from home they were a perfect outlet for her. Reasonably quick to do, they needed only simple tools and a small block of side-grain cherry on pear wood, which was cut to her specifications by T. N. Lawrence in Red Lion Passage.

One of the first woodcuts Carrington made was a self-portrait, in 1916, which she thought was 'almost deserving praise'.[18] Carrington also made a great many for friends. Subjects were puns on their names or natures; themes from mythology; arcadian, in the manner of Samuel Palmer (see p. 86), or straightforwardly decorative and two-dimensional. She was always gratified when her friends liked them and they brought in a reasonable income too.

Books became one of Carrington's greatest shared pleasures with Lytton. In 1931 she wrote in her

ABOVE Woodcut, 2 April 1917

LEFT ABOVE Bookplate, 1920, woodcut

LEFT BELOW Bookplate for St John Hutchinson, 1917, woodcut

Bookplate, 1921 woodcut

Letter drawing, 19 January
1921

diary: 'As I stuck the book plates in with Lytton I suddenly thought of Sothebys and the book plates in some books I had looked at, when Lytton was bidding for a book and I thought: These books will one day be looked at by those gloomy faced book-sellers and buyers. And suddenly a premonition of a day when these labels will no longer [be] in this library came over me. I longed to ask Lytton not to stick in any more.'[19]

Lytton was very often the thought behind what Carrington did. She cut him several bookplates for his expanding library; some of them comments on their relationship. Both *Cynical Age and Youth* and *Chiron and a Pupil*, with Lytton as the wise centaur Chiron teaching his pupil Achilles the many arts, point to Lytton's role as mentor.

In 1917 Virginia Woolf took the unexpected step of commissioning Carrington to illustrate *Two Stories*, the first publication of the Hogarth Press; unexpected because her sister Vanessa Bell was the more likely choice. And Virginia was known for being unwarrantably cruel towards the younger generation of artists she called the cropheads. That Carrington had succeeded in forming a lov-ing, companionable relationship with Lytton, who had been one of Virginia's loves, inevitably tem-pered her feelings towards Carrington, and when Carrington wrote in a late sketchbook, 'A whisp-erer separatheth chief friends', she could have had in mind Virginia's early mischief making. But, nonetheless, Virginia liked and respected Carrington, writing in her diary: 'She seems to be an artist … I think Carrington cares for it genuinely, partly because of her way of looking at pictures' and Carrington admired Virginia's books, particularly *Jacob's Room*, which was so painterly.[20]

Virginia liked Carrington's four cuts immensely, thought they made the book much more interest-ing and they helped establish the house style. Lytton adored the snail and passed on Vanessa's praise: 'Tell Carrington, if she can bear to have them mentioned, that I liked her woodcuts very much – especially I think the one of the servant girl.'[21]

The Hogarth Press had only ever been meant as a hobby carried on 'in the intervals of lives that are otherwise engaged', as Virginia wrote to a dissat-isfied customer in 1924. Books were circulated among friends, but editions became oversubscribed, the operation snowballed and Carrington undertook other commissions for it. She made designs for paper wrappers using linoleum because it was easy to cut and cheap; in August 1917 she was working on lettering for Leonard and in 1921 made a woodcut for the cover of his book, *Stories of the East* (see p. 68). No doubt Carrington would have done more but the tone of Virginia's letters became haranguing when Carrington found it difficult to meet Virginia's demands, and she

wrote: 'How can I do woodblocks when for the last month … I've been a ministering angel, hewer of wood and drawer of water? Honestly Virginia since I came here I've only been able to finish a picture which I sent Monty Shearman … So you mustn't bully me.'[22] And her involvement from that point fell off, until 1931 when she prepared designs (unused) for the dust jacket of Julia Strachey's first novel, *Cheerful Weather for the Wedding*.

Carrington also furnished two other books with illustrations and prepared work for a third which was never used. In 1916 she provided two line drawings – *The Ouse, Bedford* and *Bedford High School* – for the *Memoir and Poems of A. W. St.*

Book plate c. 1917. Harry Ransom Humanities Research Center, The University of Texas at Austin

LEFT ABOVE *The Ouse, Bedford* from *Memoir and Poems of A. W. St. C. Tisdall*, VC 1916, line drawing

LEFT BELOW One of five drawings for a school edition of *Don Quixote*, published by Oxford University Press in 1922

Clair Tisdall VC; and in 1922 she illustrated the school edition of *Don Quixote* for the Oxford University Press, for whom Noel was working.

Carrington formed a lexicon of imagery for her woodcuts which she drew upon time and again, and in *Don Quixote* we have them all – the supine forms of mountains, the lollipop cypress trees of the landscape of Spain, the sculptural outline of greyhound dogs, and the conquest of light and dark.

Sadly, the pen-and-ink drawing that Carrington made for a scene from *Wuthering Heights* was never published but, as a prescient comment upon the triangles around which the rest of her life revolved, it is illuminating. A man and a woman sit over the same book, lit by two candles which disperse the immediate darkness, but no more. The woman and her companion are drawn joined like Siamese twins; the woman has immobilized her hands by slipping them inside her sleeves and her companion turns the pages. A third person sits outside this intimacy among shadows, with two sleeping hounds at his feet and a third dog upright at his back.

By 1919 Carrington was beginning to find woodcuts too 'limited in their technique, & that certain elements, as colour, will never be able to be shown'.[23] She was ready to start working with colour again.

OPPOSITE *Wuthering Heights*, c. 1919, pen and wash on paper, 20.2 × 19 (8 × 7½). Private collection

The Servant Girl, one of four illustrations for *Two Stories*, published by the Hogarth Press, 1917, woodcut

Tidmarsh Mill and Meadows, c. 1920, oil on canvas, 68.6 × 68.6 (27 × 27). Photo: Witt Library

Tidmarsh Mill 1917–1924
4 At Home – People and Place Portraiture

It was not long before Carrington and Lytton discussed the possibility of living together in the country. Lytton wrote: 'It strikes me as maniacal to live anywhere but among trees & grasses, open skies, fresh butter, wood fires & days that are empty and endless.'[1] For the time being they were both short of money and their dream could only become reality with the help of their friends. Great things were expected of Lytton and eventually happened with the publication in 1918 of *Eminent Victorians*, a set of iconoclastic biographical essays 'which introduced a new note into assessments of the departed'.[2] The book established his literary reputation overnight, secured his livelihood and made him one of the most courted and lauded men about town.

For this reason Oliver Strachey (Lytton's brother), Maynard Keynes, Harry Norton (to whom *Eminent Victorians* was dedicated) and Saxon Sydney-Turner helped form a syndicate with the idea of taking on a lease for a house that Lytton and Carrington could call home and which would be 'a communal nest for breakers of the law'.[3]

In 1917, after months scouring the southern shires, often cycling as many as fifty miles in a day on her 'iron steed', Carrington lit upon a mill house in the village of Tidmarsh, near Pangbourne in Berkshire. Having viewed it, she wrote to Lytton in rhapsodies: 'Tidmarsh Mill it is to be. It's very romantic and lovely.
Vast Big rooms, 3 in number,
2 Very big bedrooms and 4 others,
Bathroom; water closet;
very good garden and a shady grass lawn
with river running through it.
The house is very old with gables and some lattice windows. It is joining on to the Mill … Oliver etc must go and see Tidmarsh on Tuesday. Electric

light in every room. I'm wildly excited. Hooray!'[4] The syndicate approved, there were enough bedrooms for all of them and it was only sixty-five minutes on the train from London. The lease was taken on.

Carrington's parents would never have countenanced the arrangement and so she devised a system of alibis which involved 'a complicated calendar of deceptions'.[5] With the discovery of Tidmarsh the fabric of Carrington's life became the fabric of her art. Subjects were almost all to do with Tidmarsh: the housemaid Annie, the millhouse itself, the river Pang and surrounding meadows, the local inns, Lytton of course, and their numerous visitors.

Carrington took on the furnishing and decoration almost single handedly. Lytton wrote to Virginia Woolf: 'My female companion keeps herself warm by unpacking, painting, pruning the creepers, knocking in nails, etc.'[6] Carrington planned 'to buy up all the Omega club crockery and chairs';[7] Faith Henderson had promised beds; Brett had given a motley assortment of furniture and

47

River Pang and Tidmarsh Mill, c. 1919, oil on canvas. Private collection. Carrington wrote to Lytton: 'I love the smell of fallen poplar leaves and the coloured trees and Tidmarsh so passionately'

Carrington went on 'a grand looting expedition' to Hurstbourne Tarrant.[8] Her parents were moving too, back to Prestbury where Samuel had been a boy, and Carrington used every opportunity to filch furniture and roots from the garden.

Carrington had at last found her own canopy of stars and, away from the pickled air of Soho, she was in her element. She moved in on a grey November morning, the furniture had been delivered, and she could start doing things. Planting bulbs in the garden came first and then Carrington rigged up her studio in the tank room where the light was right and there were a good many shelves.

The building above the millhouse was a corn chandler's warehouse and while Carrington was working in her studio 'the Mill creaked round and at intervals the water came crashing into the tank from the pump below'.[9] Perhaps this became a distraction because she soon transferred her materials to a room adjoining her bedroom under the eaves. She put up shelves, divided into stalls to hold the different colours, used the storage space for her drawings and drying canvases, and did all the messy work of preparation up there. She then painted in a big clean room down below.

Taste is said to be the feminine of genius and a house a woman's profits. A great deal of Carrington's creative energies went into beautifying her houses and in Tidmarsh Mill Carrington established the legacy of her taste. The atmosphere

OPPOSITE *Hoeing* (detail), 1912, one of three frescoes at Ashridge House, Berkhamsted, 1.83 × 1.52 m (6 × 5 ft). Ashridge Management College

Carrington created through taste, geniality and an affectionate nature, albeit ephemeral, had just as much genius in it as an oil painting.

The decoration of a house, and its accumulated souvenirs, is like the painting of a picture but on a different scale and more slowly achieved. The sense of colour and balance and character which makes a painter's work identifiably her own is no less apparent when painted on a wall. Few artists can paint 'serious' pictures on easels all of the time and most have found outlets or diversions for those moments.

As working at the Omega had shown, decoration and easel painting fed one another. When Carrington wrote to Lytton: 'The havoc wrought in my loneliness is great. The entire house now resembles a painting by Barbara Strachey' (Oliver's five-year-old daughter) it sounds as if working in a large way had encouraged a loosening up and the frame of mind in which Carrington painted life-sized naked figures of Adam and Eve on the walls of Lytton's bedroom.[10]

Only black-and-white photographs of Carrington's decorations at Tidmarsh remain, but we can piece together a jigsaw of what made it unique, from Carrington's descriptions in her letters, her paintings and the recollections of friends who have said that Carrington decorated the walls like a bower-bird.

Carrington was greatly moved by the English tradition of not-too-grand country-house living. Before she found Tidmarsh, Carrington wrote to Lytton describing a Jacobean house she had fantasized about living in one day. It had 'a black-lead wall painted all over with a pattern of white flowers by hand! … [and] traces of red walls with yellow patterns'.[11] It seems highly likely that something of this sensibility, found in Combe House, made its way into Tidmarsh Mill. It also explains why Carrington was so won over in 1919 by Daisy Ashford's tale of *The Young Visiters*, in which the nine-year-old storyteller described an old English interior: 'an oak door with some lovely swans and bull rushes painted on it … a handsome compartment with purple silk curtains … a dainty room all in pale yellow and wild primroses.'[12] These schemes could just as well have been of Carrington's own devising.

The Boot Boy, c. 1913, oil on canvas, 44.5 × 35 (17½ × 13¾). Private collection

Lytton Strachey, 1916, oil on canvas, 68.6 × 73.6 (27 × 29). Private collection

Frank Prewett, 1920, oil on canvas, 56 × 36 (22 × 14¼). Private collection

OPPOSITE *David Garnett*, 1919, oil on canvas, painted in Lytton's library at Tidmarsh Mill. Richard Garnett

52

'Rouen Ware', c. 1923, oil,
ink and silver foil on glass,
26.2 × 20 (10¼ × 7¾).
Private collection

OPPOSITE *Tulips in a*
Staffordshire Jug, c. 1921, oil
on canvas, 71 × 66
(28 × 26). Private
collection

sale, and 'Lytton bought on my advice a most lovely bedspread, Queen Anne embroidery with a big sun flower in the middle, very pale colours, with flowers embroidered all over it. It is a vision of delight.'[16]

Lytton's library was wallpapered with hand-printed papers, by Carrington's Slade friend Fanny Fletcher and had French windows looking out over the Pang. Duncan Grant's *Juggler and Tightrope Walker* of 1918 hung there and the curtains, from photographs, look hand-printed with a large paisley pattern seen in Carrington's tinselled picture of *Tulips*.

Carrington knew all the best antique shops and her most treasured possessions came from Mr Jarvis' curiosity room in Newbury. Carrington's finds filled her homes. Bristol blue glass and cracked but exquisite eighteenth-century porcelain found themselves neighbours with copper lustre, Staffordshire figures and Mocha ware. These 'little darlings' were objects to use and if a favourite piece was broken it was riveted back together again. Botanical books were bought from the Birrell & Garnett bookshop and Audubon birds were bid for at auction. Theatrical tinselled portraits were as prized as Aubusson carpets. Old stuffs and shell boxes, the gift of a rare Peruvian tile of a bird, comprised the fabric of her domestic life and furnished the inspiration for her painting.

Carrington housed some of this collection in her dining-room dresser. The dresser was painted yellow and the doors were decorated in pinks and greens using motifs from Rouen ware. The top was reserved for teapots and jugs for holding flowers. In the middle were Gerald Brenan's large sunny platters from Spain which he had carried for Carrington on his back across the Pyrenees, and the 'lovely pink primitive house dish' he had given her.[17] On the bottom shelf she placed three 'amazingly beautiful' sixteenth-century dark olive green wine flasks she had found in her mother's cellars; one with a glass seal of '3 wild geese, and a hand rampant'.[18]

The dresser was not the first piece of furniture Carrington had painted; she had decorated a commissioned tin trunk with 'sportive youths, and pages with greyhounds in the arches'. Some of the subjects she used were clearly chosen to titilate

Tidmarsh became a place of warmth and hospitality, 'really ... the Carlton in its comforts'.[13] 'Fires crackled on brick hearths. The wallflower's sweet scent pervaded every room. Tulips shone on a clean yellow cloth in the dining room.'[14]

Colour and sensation were everything; Carrington wrote to Lytton of her pleasure in imagining him in 'that little painted room of many colours'.[15] Carrington's own bedroom had a blue cupboard and blue chintz curtains, while the bed in a pink room was covered with a tapestry that Gerald Brenan brought back from Spain. Lytton's bedroom had a four-poster bed, purchased in a local

Tidmarsh Mill, c. 1918, oil on canvas, 64 × 94.5 (25¼ × 37¼). Private collection

both herself and Lytton, and when she described: 'I saw some good Cretan Figures in the Museum and, oh Lytton, Antinous! What a catamite to possess!' she knew they could rhapsodize over the fair forms together.[20]

The millhouse had low ceilings and not a great deal of picture-hanging room because most of the walls were lined with the coloured spines of Lytton's vast library, which also had the advantage of insulating Tidmarsh and making it beautifully snug and warm. The pictures they did have were chosen by Carrington, who had a proper reverence for another artist's work, and bought by Lytton. As well as the work of their friends, Duncan and Vanessa, they bought hand-coloured engravings of mountains and seascapes, and 'treacle' prints of *Prudence and Justice*, from the Reading antique

shops. And with Augustus John, Gertler and John Nash, Carrington made exchanges.

Because of Lytton, Carrington has always been billetted with the Bloomsbury painters, when in fact, artistically, her allegiances were with Chelsea. Carrington was excited by the atmosphere Duncan and Vanessa created at their Sussex farmhouse, Charleston, but also found it rather shambolic. The decoration at Charleston was built up into a homogeneous whole with few margins between. Carrington's decorations were more refined and designed to fit a particular place rather than to cover a whole area. She would later write that she suspected Fry found them 'too finickery & elegant'.[21]

The garden, as much as the house, helped create the feeling for Carrington that Tidmarsh was an

56

earthly paradise. She wrote: 'I really get so much pleasure from having many cats to look at on the lawn. Really they are very like the Russians [Ballet Russe]. They move so beautifully … The beauty of that garden fills me more and more.'[22] The garden was both sides of a sluiced stream off the river Pang. There was an orchard upstream with apple trees and cherry, for which Carrington got a rattle to scare off the birds; a meadow that had to be scythed; a vegetable patch; grass lawns; a lean-to 'greenery-house' for cultivating and wintering; a 'Roman bath' for outdoor bathing and a flower garden enclosed in box hedges which meant there were always flowers for cutting; tulips and dahlias were the favourites, but also primroses, larkspur, winter aconites, white anemones, sunflowers, crown imperials, pinks and sweet williams.

Carrington kept a number of creatures: cats, honey bees, cockerels for eating, seven hens who, she commented, 'lay vigorously seven eggs a day', a doe rabbit, ducks, and ewe lambs destined for the market place. She teased Lytton that she wanted a

Tulips, c. 1928, oil, ink and silver foil on glass. Private collection

Lytton's library at Tidmarsh Mill, c. 1918

The dining-room dresser at Tidmarsh Mill, *c.*1923

fox and a snake, but contented herself instead with a japanned display case full of the plaster variety, coiled and banded in viperish green, black and tan. And when David Garnett published his first book about the metamorphosis of a *Lady into Fox* in 1922, Carrington was enchanted, writing to him: 'you must have written it especially for me … Once I had a lovely dream about a fox and very often buzzards are my night companions.'[23]

After the Slade, Carrington rarely took full-scale figure compositions past the drawing stage and often abandoned designs – such as a composition of men gathering apples on long ladders in a tree – which she knew were good, but thought impossible to carry out. In 1922, however, she went to an inspiring series of lectures given by Roger Fry tracing the development of design and significant form. Reviewing the last year Carrington felt her work had become 'little' and after a weekend visit Fry made to Tidmarsh she decided to begin 'a composition of an interior scene in this kitchen.

Only I shall paint it very big. I do not want to tackle anything too difficult, or I know I shall then despair and give up the composition before it is finished.'[24]

Remarkably, Carrington's large sketch has survived and through a circuitous route ended up in the Fry bequest at the Courtauld Institute Galleries, where it is attributed to an 'anonymous child'. But there is little doubt this painting is by Carrington.[25]

Made on paper the size she used for the *Hill in Snow at Hurstbourne Tarrant*, Carrington carefully drew a bird's-eye view, painted with watercolour and highlighted with crosshatching in pen and ink. The considered colour scheming, the knowledge of perspective, and the squaring up of the sketch in the window (for transferring the design onto canvas), all point to far more sophistication than a child possesses.

The pink crockery on the table resembles Henri Doucet's designs for jugs with cockscomb tops for the Omega Workshops. The plaster walls are painted damson and yellow and coals burn hellishly hot in the black, open range bordered by green and ash coloured tiles. The balloon-back chairs at the table are mahogany red and similar to the ones in her studies for *The Feetbathers* (in the final painting she depicted the large wheel-back chairs from Lytton's library). The upholstered chairs are pink, spotted with red and green, and like the wing armchair in which she painted Lytton. The still life at the window, of a vase of red tulips and a blue-curtained view of a majestic tree, was a favourite theme seen in her sketchbooks in all sorts of permutations, with fruits or women replacing flowers.

The diminutive figures seem at first placed purely for compositional purposes but the configuration of the child and her adult minder hints unnervingly – knowing that Carrington was beset by nightmares of the beatings she received by her nurses as a child – at tensions between the woman and her charge, which crop up again in *Farm at*

Letter drawing, 17 December 1924

Watendlath and *On the Sands at Dawlish Warren*.[26] The moulded together, rather than held, hands, seen first in the illustration for *Wuthering Heights*, now suggest impotence.

The day would come when they would leave Tidmarsh and, years later, Carrington reminisced in her diary of her fondness for the mill: 'Tidmarsh all came back. How much I love places. I remem-

Kitchen Scene at Tidmarsh Mill, 1922, pencil, ink and gouache on paper, 56.4 × 74.9 (22¼ × 29½). Courtauld Institute Galleries, London

bered suddenly my "passion" for a certain tree in Burgess's back field. And the beauty of the mill at the back of the house and how once a kingfisher dived from the roof into the stream.'[27]

At Tidmarsh, inspiration, magic, enchantment, serenity, mystery, silence and privacy all found a loving home in Carrington's soul and in her paintings. The subjects for her pictures were all within a stone's throw of her back door. Carrington painted the views from the garden in all seasons; in the summer when the dark sombre elms and privet hedges still had their leaves and in the 'beauty of these winter mornings with the orange sun shining in the river and lighting up the tall Cézanne trees'.[28] Another day, in another mood, she painted the Pang and mill as Giotto would have seen them.

In her finest painting of *Tidmarsh Mill*, there is something decidedly unearthly about the double picture, with the darker picture in the mill pond. Carrington used an almost identical palette to that in her portrait of *Lytton Strachey*, so making these paintings companions for each other. It is as if the mill has a face: the black tunnel through which the Pang flows is a mouth, and the roof-top windows eyes. White clouds mottle the cerulean sky, or is it the other way round? There is not a breath of wind; the black swans could be ominous or portentous of good; and the reflection upon which they float in the looking-glass mill pond is another wonderland for Alice.

Carrington loved painting people; it was always a good way of getting started when she was stuck; and there were as many ways of painting portraits as there were faces. In her portrait of David Garnett, known as Bunny to his friends, Carrington made one of her most Post-Impressionistic works. Bunny was a research scientist at Imperial College when they met and particularly 'interested in the sexual lives of fungi'; his libertinism and his vivid description of Sarawak, which Carrington hoped to visit with Brett, fuelled their friendship.[29] The fact that this probably unfinished painting survived is something of a triumph, and undoubtedly because Bunny took it home with him at the end of the sitting.

Carrington took similar liberties with Annie, the good-natured maid-of-all-work, picturing her

against the kitchen shelves. Whereas Bunny's portrait had been about colour, with *Annie Stiles* (see p. 75) Carrington worked at simplifying the forms, making a monument of Annie and a perfectly splendid portrayal of her comely, sloe-eyed beauty, of which Carrington wrote: 'Annie was here to greet us last night more exquisite and seductive than ever. R[alph] was more than moved. She *is* a coquette.'[30]

Carrington was so satisfied with this portrait that she sent it for exhibition to the International in April 1921, and Gertler wrote: 'I wonder which is the most Renoir-like, your girl or mine.'[31] Renoir was a relatively recent discovery for both Carrington and Gertler and they shared Gertler's thought that: 'Since Goya there's only been Cézanne,

Cedar Tree in Burgess's back field, Tidmarsh Mill, c. 1920, oil on canvas, 68.5 × 56 (27 × 22). Courtesy: Anthony d'Offay Gallery, London

OPPOSITE *Annie in a pinny*, c. 1925, oil on canvas, 50.8 × 40.6 (20 × 16). Private collection

*Lytton in his library, Tidmarsh, c.*1922, oil on canvas, 71.1 × 53.3 (28 × 21). Private collection

Lytton in his library, Tidmarsh, preparation for woodcut, *c.* 1922, pen, ink and watercolour on paper, 12.7 × 7.5 (5 × 3). Private collection

Lytton in his library, Tidmarsh, c. 1922, woodcut. Harry Ransom Humanities Research Center, The University of Texas at Austin

Lytton Reading, Tidmarsh, c. 1920, ink and wash on paper (present whereabouts unknown)

sometimes Renoir – no one else has had that *sense of paint ... You* know what I mean.'[32] And in *Annie Stiles* Carrington achieved a warmth and tenderness in the girl's pink and pearly flesh that would have entranced Renoir.

Carrington drew and painted Lytton most of all and she loved his appearance so much there was an emptiness about the rooms and garden when he left. In her diary in 1919, Carrington described Lytton to herself: 'All his adventures and experiences are mental, and only enjoyed by himself. Outwardly it's like the life of one of the hens. Meals dividing up the day, books read in morning, siesta, walk to Pangbourne, more books. A French lesson with me, perhaps dinner. Reading aloud. Bed and hot water bottles, and every day the same apparently. But inside, what a variety, and what fantastic doings.'[33]

The Carmelite nun and mystic St Teresa of Avila once wrote how she 'thought of the Soul as resembling a Castle ... containing many rooms ... it is not everyone who ... possesses all he needs within his own dwelling'. It was Lytton's way of seeming to live inside himself which appealed to Carrington, a quality she had also loved in her father and that she would find attractive in Gerald Brenan.[34]

Carrington's three versions of *Lytton in his library* are a perfect example of the stages of a work and how a successful idea could be transformed by different media. In her oil painting there is an orderliness in the serried ranks of the books and a feeling of inertia. In the small, exquisitely drawn and coloured sketch on paper (a preparation for the woodblock), Lytton's beard merges with his tiger-striped jerkin taking root in his lap, and the books begin to slant. By the time the design has made its way into a woodcut the sense of movement is such that the bookshelves have become a stairway to heaven and form the apex of the print. It is an altogether more hieratic image which captures the essence of Lytton's physicality.

With rare exceptions the format of full-length portraits was reserved for Lytton and the elderly. This did not, however, have any correlation with canvas size; *Samuel Carrington* could fit into the head and shoulders of *Annie Stiles*. Carrington respected the dignity of age and she painted at least three women of character, from very different stations in life, but all equally regally: a Cornish farmer who could be a gypsy queen from the New Forest; Lady Strachey looking like an old empress, and Mrs Bridgeman, the housekeeper at 45 Downshire Hill, Hampstead, 'with a golden crown on her head as Queen Elizabeth!'[35]

Carrington's portrait of *Mrs Box*, whom she had met during her stays in the Marsland Valley between 1917 and 1919, is larger than any other portrait she painted. The affection she felt for her is clear from a letter: 'On the path down the hill Mrs Box appeared driving the cows; she held up both her arms and waved them, with a stick in one hand. And then ran towards me! It was delightful to see her again. She is still full of vigour and every day she fetches the cows from the marshes by the cottage and takes them back to the farm! And *she* is 72!'[36]

Carrington had a glorious sense of colour and it was her preoccupation; on a walking holiday with Noel she had been delighted to distinguish '7 distinct colours' in a rainbow.[37] Reproductions rarely show the subtleties of a colourist's work, and this is one of those paintings that you have to stand before to appreciate fully, not just for the beauty of the colours but for their juxtaposition.

Lady Strachey, 1920, oil on canvas, 76.2 × 60.9 (30 × 24). Scottish National Portrait Gallery

Carrington's second aim was to get the forms simplified and her painting of Mrs Box shows an affinity with what Gertler was striving for in his portraits of his mother.

Carrington's painting of Lytton's mother, the head of the Strachey clan, was one of her few portrait commissions, for which she received the goodly sum of £25. Carrington described her impressions of 'Her Ladyship' to Lytton: 'She is superb. It's rather stupid to tell *you* this. But I was completely overcome by her grandeur, and wit. I am painting her against the bookcase sitting full length in a chair, in a wonderful robe which goes into great El Greco folds. It is lined with orange. So the effect is a very sombre picture with a black dress, and mottled cloak, and then brilliant orange edges down the front of her dress. She looks like the Queen of China, or one of El Greco's Inquisitors.'[38]

As with *Mrs Box*, our eyes are drawn to the attitude of her hands and, as a contemporary photograph shows, Lady Strachey's stabbing finger was completely characteristic. It must have been in the Grant genes because Lytton also held his fingers like that. Lady Strachey, née Grant, was the aunt of Duncan who, hearing of Carrington's coup, tried to intrude on the sitting with Vanessa and Roger. Carrington wrote to Lytton in great consternation: 'It's all very well for a nude model as a back is as good as a front. But I didn't like the idea of painting her Ladyship back view in a confusion of easels and conversation!'[39] Clearly Carrington would not have been able to hold her own and fortunately Pippa Strachey (Lytton's sister) intervened. Carrington knew that Bloomsbury did not appreciate what she was trying for in her art and she cared very much. After she had finished the painting came a mood of despond; Carrington wrote to Alix: 'Lady Strachey's portrait is apparently liked by some people, mostly the domestics ... The painters of Gordon Square rather sniff at the picture. I see I shall never fit in any "school". I am not modern enough for the French style, & too clumsy to become a New EnglisHer.'[40]

She made a stick of this to beat her back with, when another time she would see her differences as strengths. After all, as Gertler pointed out: 'as you say "We know better!"'[41] and Lytton too 'felt that [Duncan and Vanessa] were not quite perfect critics – they tend to want you to be like them, and not like yourself – which is really the only thing it's worth anyone's while to be'.[42]

Very soon the ménage at Tidmarsh changed and the happiness of Carrington's relation with Lytton became bound up with another. Rex Partridge, a Major at the age of twenty-three and a veteran of the war not long returned from the hell of Flanders, entered both their lives. They were introduced by John Hope Johnstone, whom Carrington had known at the Slade, and met in the summer of 1918 when Ralph, as Lytton re-christened him, was on leave. He wrote to his great friend Gerald Brenan that he had met 'a painting damsel and a great Bolshevik who would like me to strike a blow for the Cause'.[43] Gerald Brenan

described him as being 'a Roman rather than a Greek by temperament, he called up – or so I then thought – Plutarch's portrait of Mark Anthony'.[44]

Ralph could not have been more opposite to Lytton, and Carrington highlighted their differences in a drawing of them by a river. Lytton's thin frame is covered from throat to toe in suiting and shoes, his sombrero lies by his side (just in case) and he holds a parasol above his head; not an inch of ivory skin is unprotected. Ralph, lying in the sun by his side, bare but for shorts, appears immensely big and robust and exposed.

By the summer of 1919 Ralph was spending most of his weekends at Tidmarsh, digging the potato patch and sitting to Carrington for paintings. Carrington loved Lytton more than ever; Lytton was falling in love with Ralph; Ralph was in love with Carrington and each one loved the other. Ralph wanted marriage. In one of the most poignant and desperate letters Carrington ever penned, she wrote to Lytton on the eve of her wedding of the 'savage cynical fate which had made it impossible for my love ever to be used by you' and the realization that 'I never could have my Moon'.[45] Carrington married Ralph, against her will, to maintain the status quo, but would never change her maiden name. She would always be Lytton's 'loving Carrington'. Lytton replied: 'My dearest and best, ... You and Ralph and our life at Tidmarsh are what I care for most in the world – almost (apart from my work and some few people) the *only* things I care for.'[46] And he trod on the heels of this letter by joining them in Venice for their honeymoon.

None of the several portraits Carrington painted of Ralph has survived. She wrote to Noel of the difficulties she was having with one in particular, of Ralph dressed as a boxer: 'But I fear I shall not carry it through its becoming rather difficult to manage. The paint gets too thick & the colours dirty after one has worked at the picture for very long I find.'[47] The problem for an artist has always been knowing when to leave a picture alone.

Many of Carrington's paintings are lost, too many to list. The irony is that having been so delighted by *The Young Visiters* she thought it one of the great tragedies of the century that so many of Daisy Ashford's stories perished through carelessness.

5 The English Tradition of Popular Art

In 1978, when Christ Church Picture Gallery in Oxford mounted a retrospective of Carrington's paintings, decorations and drawings, the porters boasted to Noel that the first Saturday was like St Giles' Fair Day. Rather extraordinary for somebody who balked at the prospect of a one-woman show but who, nonetheless, would have liked the simile because Carrington thought 'all that is best in English life congregates at a fair'.[1]

The rising appreciation of folk art in Britain is generally pinpointed to 1951, when British character and tradition were celebrated in the Lion and the Unicorn Pavilion at the Festival of Britain. That same year the Architectural Press published *The Unsophisticated Arts* drawn and described by Barbara Jones, and Enid Marx and Margaret Lambert brought out their book *English Popular Art*. All three events appeared to be pioneering because, unlike the Americans, the English generally dismissed folk art as being uncultured. But Carrington loved English naive art and knew that even in her time the sub-cultures, on which the local peculiarities of folk art rested, were disappearing.

One could never call Carrington a naive painter, if only for the simple reason that she was a trained artist. But whereas Carrington's contemporaries looked to the primitive art of Africa, Carrington was more drawn to the peasant art of Europe and America; when Augustus John visited America in 1928 Carrington advised him to look at the primitive wall paintings at Clark House in Boston. And there is a quality in her applied art, and some of her fine art, of what is described by the not wholly satisfactory term of popular art. On 1 February 1915 Carrington went to the World's Fair at Islington with a party of friends. Wandering around the sideshows David Garnett described how they came to where 'the Tattooed Venus exhibited herself ...

The World's Fair at Islington, 1915 (l to r): John Nash, David Garnett, Vanessa Bell, Oliver Strachey, Carrington, Duncan Grant, Barbara Bagenal

Her entire back, from the very cleft of her bottom to the nape of her neck and her shoulders and arms were marvellously emblazoned with mermaids, sea serpents, ships in full sail, sailors, tigers, elephants with howdahs, British soldiers in scarlet coats and spiked helmets assailed by natives armed with assegias, all intertwined with whorls of red and blue and black so as to give the effect of a Paisley shawl inspired by the chapter headings in *Petit Larousse*.

'Carrington was spell-bound and gazed at her in silence for a little while. Then, to my horror, I saw her wet her finger with her saliva and rapidly rub a spot on the living tapestry before us. The Venus turned on her indignantly and Carrington at once said: "I beg your pardon ... I forgot that you were ..."'[2]

Carrington's artistic sensibilities were inspired by several things: the poetry of the commonplace of John Clare; the oriental dragons of the tattooing

Tiles painted for a fireplace surround in Noel Carrington's Hampstead home, c. 1930. By kind permission of Spink & Son Ltd, London

'Professors'; the 'demountable baroque' of the fairgrounds and circus; the art of the mariners'; the rose and castle of the canal boats and the signboard painters. In fact most of the things pictured on the back of the tattooed Venus. They all gave form to her love of the country, country matters and 'things made to country needs and tastes'.[3]

Carrington began painting signboards in 1916 and held the art in high esteem, as she wrote to Lytton: 'Did you ever see in the hall of Bunny's house a picture belonging to Miss Bulley, of a groom with a horse and a dog? It is a terrific masterpiece, belonging to that late eighteenth-century school of English sign painters.'[4] In 1921 she painted her first inn sign for the Tidmarsh inn, picturing *The Greyhound* standing like a prize-winning dog at a show. Three further commissions were given to her on the strength of it and she wrote: 'If the Brewery will stump up £10 a sign I'll be content to be their painter for the rest of my life'.[5]

She was also painting signboards for Pangbourne shopkeepers and told Gerald Brenan that it was 'a greater honour to my mind than becoming a member of the London Group'.[6] Perhaps when she wrote to Lytton 'I painted my roebuck all today. I want to get rid of it and start some serious work'[7] she was looking for more of the reassurance that Lytton had already given her when she began painting signs in 1916, and he had written: 'I do love your sketch of the sign-board. How the diable do you manage to bring about such powerful neatness? But I will say no more, as you'll no doubt refuse to believe it.'[8]

Carrington painted *The Roebuck* against a background of miniature mountains clotted with farmlands, combining the elements of the cool, silvery blue landscapes of Joachim Patenier that she loved, and the one that Samuel Butler had painted himself against *c.* 1873.

In 1923 Carrington painted the signboard of The Spreadeagle in Thame, Oxfordshire for John Fothergill. It was based upon his sketch and unlike anything Carrington would have designed. But to be invited to paint the sign was an honour, for The Spreadeagle was a unique place: the clientele it attracted made it a little Chelsea in Thame and Fothergill was a legend in his lifetime. Fothergill had been at the Slade in the 1890s but had given up painting in 1922 to be what had previously been thought incompatible, a gentleman *and* an innkeeper. At The Spreadeagle he mingled the

The Greyhound, signboard for the Tidmarsh inn, 1921

LEFT Letter drawing, 21 February 1917

FAR LEFT *The Roebuck*, signboard for inn at Tilehurst, 1922

BELOW Signboard for The Spreadeagle, Thame, c.1923

ambience of Boswell's England with the colour of the modern French.

In eighteenth-century England, when illiteracy was rife, picture signs were a common sight swinging from the upper stories of the high street. Hogarth, Richard Wilson and Millais had all painted trade signs and a great deal of fuss was made in the iron framing of them. The fine wrought ironwork which framed Carrington's sign was already an anachronism in Carrington's day. Her sign was originally hung fifteen feet out over the parapet on iron bars and tie rods, but in 1926, after ninety-two years of swinging, it was no longer safe and a free-standing replacement was made.

The eighteenth-century sign painters were generally self-taught itinerant artists who could turn their hands to most things, be it graining, marbling, simulating tortoiseshell, or painting 'furnishing' pictures. These pictures were generally horizontal designed to fit the area of panelling between the high fireplaces and low ceilings common in inns. As with Carrington's *Kitchen Scene* they were often characterized by an absence of shadows, and an odd perspective, which allowed for the panoramic views they contained.

Carrington made decorative pictures like these when she furnished her own homes. She also made them for her friends. Pictures were generally painted on canvas and hung in the appointed place or painted in situ when they were part of a larger decorative scheme. For Marjorie Strachey, she of the pince-nez, Carrington made a large canvas, approximately 2′ by 3′, for the overmantel at Rookfield on Fridays Hill, Surrey. The theme of the picture was a formal parkland, of the kind that Arthur Devis placed his patrons in, with a peacock sitting on a stone balustrade; a three-tier fountain; an avenue of trees and tulips; a plump cat and the disappearing back of a Balthusian visitor.

By the nineteenth century fairgrounds had become elaborate attractions. Barbara Bagenal had a traditional gypsy caravan and Carrington painted a large picture on plywood of *The Gypsie Horse Stealers* for the interior. The gypsy caravans and the showmen's roundabouts and carousels were magnificently crafted, painted and gilded, using the ornamental skills of the carvers of ships' figure-heads and the flamboyance of the Chinese circus. The circus too was coming into its own with menageries of 'wild' animals being shown in hippodromes. Carrington pictured every single one of these things in her art.

Carrington sometimes stayed at Oliver Strachey's house in South Hill Park, Hampstead, and in 1917 she painted the bank-holiday funfair on Hampstead Heath from her window, describing it to Lytton: 'divinely lovely soldiers plugging at cocoanuts! – Lying in the sun circles of people. Like the apostles in that picture by Bellini – making amazing groups. Young caravan lurchers with Brass buttons on their coats fast asleep with shiney red faces & fair eyelashes … Then near the Vale there were under the tall trees wonderful lemonade mongers with Bright Blue carts & mounted on the top huge glass bowls of gamboque yellow liquid with lemons on a grate to persuade the audience that the liquid was the result of pressure on the side of a lemon! … Then we went on the merry go rounds near the Vale of Heath Publick. Round & Round Three times without getting off. My hair creating hostile yells from the populace below … when we have that grand house with immense gardens I shall have a merry go

round erected & sit on an ostrich, only tunes will *never* repeat & the machine will go on as long as I want it to.'[9]

In Carrington's watercolour *Fairground at Henley Regatta* 'Cézanne' trees front the scene and people stroll among pyjama-striped awnings; English gallopers can be seen and the panels of the rounding boards on the rides are painted with a Rousseauesque scene, which may also have been inspired by *Green Mansions*, W. H. Hudson's romance of the tropical forest.

Carrington sketched the Lippizaner horses going through their displays of *haute école* when she visited Austria in February 1922. Closer to home Carrington made a painting in miniature, framed outwardly with simple white passepartout painted brown, and inwardly with painted tableau curtains, drawn back and up in theatrical drapes like in a toy theatre, behind which marionette riders performed feats of daring-do on the table-top backs of dressage horses.

By the nineteenth century the fine porcelain figures found in elegant eighteenth-century houses had made their way into cruder versions as 'image toys' and mantelpiece ornaments which most cottagers could afford. Geoffrey Nelson, Carrington's companion at the fair on Hampstead Heath, gave her two Staffordshire figures of Prince Charlie and Prince Albert, which she loved. And when Carrington was staying at Mrs Elford's boarding

Circus Horses, mid 1920s, oil on canvas, 33 × 73.6 (13 × 29). Photo: Family Copies

Beeny Dogs, 1917, oil on canvas, 68.5 × 54.5 (27 × 21½). Private collection

house, Beeny Farm, near Boscastle in Cornwall, she painted her *Beeny Dogs*: 'two china dogs on the mantlepiece. Marvellous creatures, white with salmon pink noses'.[10] Mrs Elford's shiny boot-black mantelshelf embellished with Victorian plush, could never be confused with Carrington's home, but with the dogs, the decorated oil lamp and the old framed print, the arrangement had the formula that Carrington responded to.

The Kennet canal, where Carrington used to bathe in the summer and skate in the winter, linked the river Avon at Bath with the river Thames and Reading. She would have noticed the reflex painting on the narrow boats: cabin doors always had a 'castle' which looked like a Russian church, a bridge over a stretch of water and often two swans or a boatman, as if to persuade us that the water was really wet. In a triumphant set of tiles painted to celebrate the marriage in November 1929 of her friends Alec and Frances Penrose, Carrington painted a genealogy in pictures, interspersed with poular motifs taken from canal boats and sailors' scrimshaw work on stay busks.

Carrington painted forty-five tiles in all, in yellow and violet on white. For every family portrait, such as Grandfather Peckover's country seat, Aunt Algerina's cat, Bombie the Spaniel, and the hermit owl in the shell grotto at Sibalds Holme, Carrington devised a motto such as 'No Pen without a Rose', a flaming sun with a genial face, a song bird on a leafy bough, a sailing ship in full rig and

entwined initials and hearts. At the top Carrington painted mixed flowers in goblets and jugs from her own dresser and surmounted the whole with roped-up tableau curtains.

In the same vein, and in imitation of the eighteenth-century paper cut-out silhouettes made with a physiognotrace, Carrington painted two *Fancy Ancestors* for the Penroses, each eyelash and piece of gold-lace fichu meticulously defined with black paint on the reverse of glass.

Carrington painted hundreds of tiles for her homes and those of her friends. She bought white blanks from Maw & Co., painting her design onto the biscuit base and then sending them away to be glazed and fired. A set with a hunt theme which she made in October 1927 for Margaret Waley's Dial House in Littlehampton was first prepared in a watercolour sketch and squared-up for painting onto 3-inch tiles. The next year Carrington described watching a hunt meet and following them on foot through a wood, delighting in the sight of the 'Fat Rowlandson ladies … bouncing along on their fat horses. Farmers with elbows sticking out' and, like Rowlandson's comments upon eighteenth-century manners, Carrington, *more suo*, showed twentieth-century country life with the very English feel for landscape that is associated with Gainsborough.[11] And, just as eighteenth-century furnishing pictures were painted to the bevelled edges of the panelling they fitted, the trees reach right to the edges of the picture plane.

The Hunt, fireplace tile design, 1927, watercolour on paper

Black Swan, 1917, woodcut for Montague Shearman

Fireplace tiles painted for the marriage of Alec and Frances Penrose, 1930

Tile design for Penrose fireplace surround, 1930

OPPOSITE *Mrs Box*, 1919, oil on canvas, 91.4 × 76.2 (36 × 30). Private collection

74

Fairground at Henley Regatta, c. 1921, watercolour on paper, 33 × 43.2 (13 × 17). Courtesy: Anthony d'Offay Gallery, London

OPPOSITE *Annie Stiles,* 1921, oil on canvas, 50.8 × 40.6 (20 × 16), painted in the kitchen at Tidmarsh Mill. David Evers

75

Gerald Brenan at Larrau,
1922, oil on canvas. Private
collection

Farm at Watendlath, 1921,
oil on canvas, 60.9 × 68.6
(24 × 27). Tate Gallery,
London

Yegen 'landscape', 1924, oil on canvas, 68.6 × 78.7 (27 × 31). Private collection

Spanish Boy, c. 1924, oil on canvas, 63.5 × 50.8 (25 × 20). Private collection

Larrau Snowscape, 1922, oil on canvas, 30.4 × 40.6 (12 × 16). Private collection

6 An Expanding World – At Home and Abroad

On walking and motoring tours in the 1920s Carrington discovered the entire pageant of England and after the home-inspired scenes of Tidmarsh Mill began to paint emotive landscapes, great expanses of silent territory, which hint at her view of the status of people in the true scheme of things. These paintings have a profound and poetic quality which show that Carrington brought the whole of her psychological make-up to bear on them, but also hint at the stimulation she felt, stepping up onto an emotional high wire, when she met Gerald Brenan.

As Virginia Woolf foretold, Carrington's marriage was more risky than most. Without considering it any threat, Ralph took other lovers almost instantly, and by 1921 Carrington had started a private correspondence with Gerald, Ralph's best friend.[1] Carrington first met Gerald, with Ralph, in May 1919 during his annual return to England from Spain. But John Hope Johnstone, Brenan's boyhood friend, had described Carrington to Gerald in 1915, even before Ralph had known her, and had so fired his imagination that he spent the war years dreaming about her. Gerald wrote: 'She had become the symbol of the kind of girl I wanted to know' and when he was in England in 1917 recovering from wounds he had received in France, he frequented the haunts of artists in the hope of meeting Carrington.[2]

Within six months of demobilization Gerald found himself a peasant house in a remote village in the Andalucian mountains which suited all his present needs. Spain was a country where he could settle that was cheap and congenial and where he could eke out his war bonus of £250. Initially he had no thought of becoming a writer; all he wanted was to work his way through the 2000 books he had shipped out in tea chests. He was, seemingly, immune to loneliness and boredom.

Letter drawing, April c. 1922

Carrington later wrote to Gerald: 'I am in love with Shelley and so I pretend Shelley lives in you.'[3] She also had Shelley-like cravings of her own and having met Gerald several times in the summer of 1919, suggested that they write to each other while he was in Spain. What began as the innocent correspondence of pen-friends acted as a tinder box, and their uninhibited letters became increasingly intimate and necessarily secret. By December 1919 Carrington was writing: 'I believe if one wasn't reserved, and hadn't a sense of "what is possible" one could be *very* fond of certainly two or three people at a time.'[4]

81

The relationship finally kindled into the beginnings of an affair two years later, when Carrington wrote to Gerald that 'the discovery of a person, of an affection, of a new emotion, is to me next to my painting, the greatest thing I care about' and she invited him to join her on a holiday she was planning in Cumberland.[5] On paper Gerald seemed to share her sentiments, writing: 'I do not understand the possessive instinct and I do not share it: it is part of my philosophy that love is free and unrestricted and is increased by being divided', when in fact, as his biographer Jonathan Gathorne-Hardy has pointed out, Gerald was capable of out-rivalling Othello.[6]

The paintings Carrington made of Gerald, of Watendlath Farm in Cumberland where the seeds of their affair were sown, the Pyrenean mountain village of Larrau, and the 'yellow oxhide land' of Granada, have a similar psychological power to those she painted of Lytton and Tidmarsh; her father Samuel and Hurstbourne Tarrant.[7]

Watendlath was a tiny hamlet of yeomans' dwellings, in a tree-sheltered spot with a tarn, surrounded by the lowering forms of lumpish hills which made a small world of the valley they enclosed. For a sculptural painter it was heaven. Carrington and Ralph, with Gerald, Alix, James and Lytton later, spent much of the month of August at Watendlath and Carrington painted two landscapes there, both of which show the domination of bedrock and very little sky.

The painting now in the Tate pictures the great mass of moorlands behind the farmhouse; their bald nakedness uncompromised by superfluous detail as if painted through a typical Lakeland blue-grey haze. Carrington wrote of this scene: 'I sat and drew a white cottage and a barn … sitting on a little hill until it grew too cold … The trees are so marvellously solid, like trees in some old Titian pictures, and the houses such wonderful greys and whites, and then the formation of the hills so varied.'[8]

The farmhouse blinks blindly from its gaping black windows, revealing nothing of the interior life – Carrington reserved that for her letters – except we know that it is washing day and we can imagine the popping sound as the wind catches the white sheets on the line, motions the leaves of the bent cedars, and hurries the tumbling beck over the brown-stained boulders. The mysterious quality of the now familiar linked-figures adds a white foil to balance the right-hand side of the picture, and an edge to the atmosphere too.

In the second landscape, which Carrington gave to Gerald, we have a harsher scene of scree and rocky knoll, painted using the infinite variety of greens in nature and with something of the mystic beauty of El Greco's visionary greens in *Toledo in a Storm*. But at the bottom of this wilderness, fit for St Jerome, is a benign scene of a stonewalled field of unruffled 'model' sheep of the kind you find in naive images.

Carrington painted two portraits of Gerald; for the first of which he sat in the 'yew tree barn' at Watendlath. She painted him in the workmanlike weeds he habitually wore, and with a skilful use of light captured Gerald's heart's history in his brown-eyed gaze.

Carrington's second portrait of Gerald, was painted a year on, in March, in the attic of a house at Larrau, in the French Pyrenees. It was the mountain home of Valentine and Bonamy Dobrée and the first time Carrington and Gerald had been together since Watendlath; Gerald had grown a moustache and his expression was less fulsome. Ralph had entered into a passionate involvement with Valentine, who later told him of Carrington and Gerald's intentions, and so struck the match which ignited 'the great row'.

Ralph could not tolerate the idea of Carrington having a lover, even though nothing had happened between Carrington and Gerald at that point 'except embrasades'.[9] The rules of the *ménage à trois* at Tidmarsh had been worked out as they went along and it had become a peculiarly stable arrangement. Gerald's appearance as a potential fourth was as undesirable to Ralph and Lytton as the infant cuckoo is to a neighbour's nest and Carrington found her 'Triangular Trinity of Happiness' in serious jeopardy.[10]

Although there would be a reconciliation in November, the enforced estrangement between Carrington and Gerald was almost intolerable for both of them. Gerald had reserved his '*summa inspiratio*' for Carrington and it would seem, spiritually, losing Gerald was a greater privation to

Farm at Watendlath, 1921,
oil on canvas. Private
collection

Carrington than the loss of Ralph would have been, but less than the sum of the loss of Lytton and Ralph (on whom Lytton had come to depend) and the life all three had made together at Tidmarsh.[11]

Carrington's letter to Lytton goes some way to explaining her feelings for the three men in her life and the reasons for her ultimate choice: 'I cannot but help being lonely without seeing you, and I feel so often perhaps you miss me … Victoria matters so much to me. That['s] what Ralph doesn't feel. The importance above everything [that] a work of art, and a creator of such works, has for me. And yet do you know, this morning I felt these conflicting emotions are destroying my purpose for painting. That perhaps that feeling which I have had ever since I came to London years ago now, that I am not strong enough to live

in this world of people, and paint, is a feeling which has complete truth in it. And yet when I envision leaving you and going like Gerald into isolation, I feel I should be so wretched that I should never have the spirit to work.'[12]

Carrington resumed her relationship with Gerald after the row, but it became a frustration. Although Gerald would not admit it, he wanted Carrington conclusively, and doggedly tried to break down the distances between them, the very things which had made it possible for each to see the other whole and against a wide sky. Gerald later found happiness with the poet Gamel Woolsey, but Carrington's memory was never far from him. He wrote to V. S. Pritchett in 1979: 'I was as proud of my affair with her as I was of having been in the line at Passchendaele. The tears I shed for her were, I thought, my true

83

Spain, 1920 (l to r) Ralph Partridge, Gerald Brenan, Lytton Strachey

same culture as architecture, and furniture, always reviving some style and trying to build up a mixture with dead brains. The French cover their tracks better [than] the English do. But really I don't think much of this revival of Rembrandt, nudes à la Rubens, imitations of the naive artists, Poussin. Matisse seems to me one of the most definitely original artists alive now. I think all this "culture", and "groups" system perhaps is partly the reason of the awful paintings produced.'[14]

A further difficulty was that Carrington's world was made up of several orbits that on the whole did not mix, but occasionally touched and overlapped, like a Venn diagram, when Chelsea met Bloomsbury. Carrington's creative kinship had always been with Gertler, Nash, John, and later Henry Lamb, Boris Anrep and Simon Bussy.[15]

And whereas Carrington had been a faithful disciple of Fry, by 1927 she was seriously questioning the 'brahmin of Bloomsbury',[16] writing to Gerald 'I trust your taste a hundred times more than Roger's'.[17] Her friends agreed. Gertler felt 'how terribly misled one has been all along by the "wizards' and intellectuals'" interpretations ... I mean Roger Fry & Co.'[18] And in June 1923 Bussy wrote in the Nation that Grant had 'a manner of using paint which makes the canvas look more like stuff that has been dipped in a dye than like a painted picture'.[19]

Lytton felt it was essential for Carrington to show her pictures if she was to find some independence. But, like Emily Dickinson, Carrington was reluctant to 'invest her snow'. Carrington had exhibited her work erratically since leaving the Slade. She did not want to align herself with any current asylum of thought and the aesthetic consciousness was so universally undeveloped that when she did show her work it was either apathetically received – as in 1920 when she exhibited three paintings with the London Group – or criticized, as Carrington described: 'There is arrant bilge written in this week's Nation and Athenaeum ... What a pass things have come to! No one can just enjoy with their eyes simply, they must argue and reason and criticise.'[20]

But most damaging of all was Carrington's self censor and her unwarranted feeling that her work did not match her expectations. George Rylands

medals', and Gerald dreamt about Carrington until the 1950s, keeping the green dress she wore at Watendlath and a lock of her hair until he died.[13]

Carrington could have painterly conversations with Gerald and she wrote to him: 'But I can't see the use of painting pictures "as good as" those at the London Group. I think except for a few French artists, and perhaps two English artists there are NO important LIVING artists. Painting hasn't advanced, there are very few inventors and original artists alive now. They reduce painting to the

would say of Carrington that 'she was as self deprecating as a domestic pussy cat, almost incapable of self-praise'.[21]

Carrington was acclaimed for her work by those whose opinions she valued. Lytton passed on the eulogistic praise of his brother-in-law, Simon Bussy after he saw Carrington's paintings at Tidmarsh: '"Better than anything at the London Group ... Better than most French things – better than Marchand 'et tous ces gens' – much"! ... There was no doubt about the genuineness of it all.'[22] And the year before, in the summer of 1919, when André Derain was in London with Picasso to oversee a production of Diaghilev's *La Boutique Fantasque*, Gertler wrote to S.S. Koteliansky: 'I hear by the way that when Derain was taken round the London Group he picked out, without knowing the name, pictures by Roger Fry as being the best. Also at a party he saw a picture by Carrington and thought it excellent. So that Roger Fry and Carrington are the two best English artists, according to Derain.'[23]

And in May 1921 Fry selected Carrington's painting of tulips for The 'Nameless Exhibition of Modern British Painting' which had 'Representative Works of all Contemporary Movements including Royal Academicians & the Extreme Moderns'. All pictures were being shown anonymously until the last fortnight, when the names of the painters were divulged, which certainly would have appealed to Carrington, and the exhibition opened on 20 May, the day before Carrington married Ralph.

But, as Fry's story relayed to Vanessa Bell proved, women artists still had to duck male prejudice: 'Tonks [visiting the exhibition] gave a little lecture on what a pity that women always imitated men', when he had in fact mistaken a Bell for a Grant, finding Vanessa's painting of *Three Women in a Conversation* the superior work.[24] And patrons for women were hard to find; the collector Edward Marsh was unparalleled in the financial and emotional encouragement he gave, but it was almost exclusively to male painters.

In 1918 Carrington had written to Gertler about Fry: 'He is one of the *best* people I think. As he really cares so much for good work. And is aloof from criticising people for their personal weak-

nesses and characters',[25] and Fry considered Carrington one 'of our lot'.[26] It therefore comes as some surprise that when Carrington approached Fry for advice about her work he is said to have dissuaded her from pursuing a career as an artist. This story is hearsay (passed down by Ralph) and may be apocryphal, but it is known that Fry was blinded by the French to the merits of the English tradition that so obviously informed Carrington's work, and that taste and prejudice are dangerously alike.

In 1918 Carrington's father died, leaving her a legacy which gave her an annual income of £130. It did not quite match up to Virginia Woolf's stipulation of £500 a year and a room of one's own, but it provided Carrington with a small measure of financial independence and, most importantly, it was an acknowledgement by her father of her complete seriousness as a painter.

The Gerald rumpus was a pivotal time in Carrington's life. Living and loving creatively had thrown up the age-old conflict: 'You know I think it's very difficult to live quite by myself. I keep on pretending I am GOD but it all seems rather a deception ... I can't quite make myself do anything for myself, eating seems tiresome, and one lies in a chair dreaming of colours, and pulling out visions, instead of eating tea ... I wonder if it is a fundamental difference between female and male – this GOD business and one's disinterestedness in oneself.'[27]

Carrington felt enormously chastened by her experience with Gerald and what Lytton once called the 'vertigo of ever-intensifying complications'[28] which had come about through having 'plural affections'. But the resulting moratorium brought about a new and fierce determination for her art. In June 1922 in a letter-diary to Gerald during the schism Carrington wrote: 'If I become a very good painter no one can take that from me and today I feel rather proud, rather moved from everyone, even cynical about myself, except that I wish to paint very well.'[29] She knew that: 'The solution to all my difficulties lies up stairs in my studio'[30] and that 'I mind none of the vexations of life when I am painting'.[31]

Travelling, and the stimulation of it, was part of the answer and she found it compelling. After four

Letter drawing, 15 February 1922

years of war the opportunities for travel were as limitless as Carrington's will to do so. The outlines of native trees and vernacular architecture abroad were so different from what the eye yielded at home that she acquired a store of completely new images. Up until this point Carrington had mostly known the work of the great painters through reproduction. Now she could feast upon them in the magnificent galleries of Europe and in the myriad churches and government houses of Italy and Spain.

The seeds of an allegiance were sown. Carrington wrote to Lytton from Madrid: 'This morning I spent in the Prado. How can one say what one feels when all the air has been pressed out of one's lungs through the sheer exhaustion of marvelling. The portraits of Goya perhaps delighted me as much as anything.'[32] And from Paris to Gerald: 'I came to a great many agitating conclusions at the Louvre this morning. A conflict always arises in reconciling my passion for the early Sienese or the very early Florentine with the amazing solidity of Titian and Giorgione. I tremble over the delicate beauty of those little panels, the naive simplicity of their designs and the colour they are, but when I see Titian and El Greco their powerful intellectual designs make me stand still … When I am at the Louvre I suddenly feel so certain of myself. I feel there is nothing to prevent my painting my now fervent image of the nymph who turned into a stag so perfectly that it could be no disgrace.'[33]

Although Bilbao looked 'very like what one conceives a south American port run up in 2 weeks by a cinema firm would be',[34] when Carrington visited Gerald in his mountain fastness at Yegen for the first time in March of 1920 she found it a 'unique arcadia' and had 'seldom been so happy continuously day after day'.[35] In Granada she bought small canvases approximately 12 inches by 16 inches for ease of travelling, and painted most afternoons attended by a little village girl of twelve who sat beside her holding her paint box.

Granada was a province of contrasts and Carrington painted all aspects of it: the white hill towns of shoebox houses, with flat roofs the colour of blue corn, on grey-green hillsides, and the Alpujarras, which Gerald described: 'the chief charm of both Mecina and Yegen is the view – perhaps the most

beautiful in the world. At one's feet in the "plain" or rather basin of Ugíjar are row upon row of desert hills, rounded, carved and shaped by wind and water, covered with little bushes or else with almond trees. Beyond is the coast range, through a broad gap in which one sees the sea – some forty miles away … but [the mountains] are not steep or jagged. They are wonderfully modelled by a network of gullies and ravines … which, if I could draw, I would like to draw all day.'[36]

On a walk along the spine of a high ridge of mountains from Orgiva to Yegen, Carrington had seen Africa through the cork forests and set her sights upon going there. For Bunny's birthday on 9 March 1923 she had given him an 1822 illustrated edition of Mungo Park's *Travels in the Interior of Africa*, and she sailed to Tunis with Lytton and Ralph that same month, making several drawings at Hammam-Meskoutine, which she painted up on her return to England.

Carrington's most visionary and surreal painting was made of Gerald's view, and the sea that separated Spain from the Moors, in an intensely cold English March when snow lay on the ground. Carrington felt that 'Doré, or Blake could hardly have conceived anything more frenzied' and, improvizing from a store of remembered images, Carrington painted her 'Yegen "landscape"' with a poetic quality even more profound and disquieting than the real thing.[37] The painting transported her into another world and she wrote to Gerald: 'I cannot express quite the relief it is.' She tried 'a new plan, an entire underpainting in brilliant colours, over which I shall glaze green and more transparent colours'.[38]

The brilliancy of the colours obtained through glazing could be superb, but was an elaborate working process and also unpredictable. The more usual and simpler method of painting with oils was to put down the correct tone and colour with freshly mixed paint, but with glazing the build up of layers of transparent colours meant that the finished work was the result of several paintings. It could take months to complete because each layer of paint needed to be fairly dry before it could be worked over.

Carrington's painting of the ruthlessly bare sunset mountains, coloured and marked like the fruit of the prickly pear, has the imaginative intensity of Sassetta's *Flagellation of St Anthony*. But whereas Sassetta's landscape was purely background to the tormenting demons, in Carrington's painting it is primary. So dominant is the sensation of the mountains (like giants' 'knees under bedclothes'), the pimply volcanic eruptions and the primordial-looking century plants, it comes as some surprise to see the tiny almond trees, and the road carved into the hillside with its four muleback riders.[39]

Gerald often had musical gatherings at his house in the evenings and Carrington must have asked a boy who played a squeeze box to sit for his portrait in Gerald's dining room. This painting has a marvellous sense of dark and light, achieved with very little variation of colour, and a current of mood passing through it which is clearly a homage to El Greco and his portrait of the poet Fray Hortensio Felix Paravicino.

The sketchbooks Carrington travelled with are full of complex compositions of villages, fields and trees which stand as finished works by themselves, but which would never make their way into paintings, because she favoured simplification with colour.

In Larrau in 1922, as well as the portrait of

Mountain church, Larrau, 1922, oil on canvas, 37 × 37 (14½ × 14½). Private collection

Vermenton, 1923, oil on canvas, 26 × 20.2 (10¼ × 8). Private collection

French Boys, c. 1929, black chalk on paper, 34.5 × 25 (13½ × 9¾). Private collection

In 1923 Lytton attended a conference in France and Carrington and Barbara Bagenal went along for the trip. They stayed at the Hotel du Commerce in the Romanesque town of Vermenton on the Yonne, which Carrington painted at the end of the day when the shadows were long and the town's Lilliputian inhabitants were out, writing to Lytton: 'I was so excited at painting again. Do you know I am never quite so happy as when I can paint. Everything else seems to fade miraculously.'[40]

Carrington's exquisite painting of a Mediterranean seascape offers a warm contrast to the chilly scenes of the French interior and evokes the sensations described by Joseph Campbell: 'When a fortunate rhythm has been struck by an artist, you experience a radiance and are held in aesthetic arrest.' The onlooker 'trembles' before this canvas just as Carrington did over the delicate beauty of the early Sienese. One can only hazard a guess at when or where this and its companion piece were painted, but perhaps they were made in September 1929 when Carrington went on a boozing, epicurean holiday around the Côte d'Or and cathedral towns of France with Dorelia and Augustus John, and two Siamese cats.

Gerald, Carrington painted two views of the mountain village: one after a flurry of snow which capped the curved roofs typical of the Pays Basque, the other in its delicate early March colours. In both pictures the buildings have the commanding aspect. Except for the sturdy black crosses in the graveyard representing the souls buried there, the snowscene is unpeopled. In the closer view of the church the impact of two challenging, crow-black figures far outweighs their tiny size in the picture plane; and their sermonizing stances are ominous portents of the discovery of Carrington's love for Gerald.

Cézanne believed that 'when colour has its richness, form has its plenitude'. In Carrington's painting of a fishing boat she jettisoned physical exactitude in favour of a heavenly procession of colours, allowing colour to define form. Painted as if through a sun-induced squint, which filters out overmuch detail – no signboards or people here –

Carrington also used the lessons of Cézanne's 'cylinder, sphere and cone' theory: the horizontal lines of the fishing boat give breadth to the picture; the perpendicular lines of the carousel mast and large sail give depth; and the abalone colours for the ocean suggest all the chambers in the heart of the sea.

Fishing Village in the Mediterranean, c. 1929, oil on paper, 23.8 × 29.5 (9⅛ × 11⅝). Courtesy: Anthony d'Offay Gallery, London

Downs from Ham Spray in winter, 1929–30, oil on canvas, 30.5 × 35.6 (12 × 14). Private collection

Ham Spray 1924–1932
7 A Green World – Conversation Pieces

By 1923 Tidmarsh had become a 'tomb of funguses', too cramped and too damp for book lovers. These Ibsenesque qualities, as Carrington saw them, together with the millhouse rats who made a meal of her portfolio of drawings, meant it was time to move.[1] They were in earnest, and with Lytton's new prosperity there was the opportunity to buy somewhere. *Country Lifes* piled up, and Carrington wrote: 'Our sitting room resembles a dentist's waiting room.'[2]

Carrington was an emotional property owner and found that property in Ham Spray House. She wrote to Gerald: 'Yesterday we saw a house upon which all my hopes now centre' and went on to describe their first impressions: 'we saw a ram shackle lodge, a long avenue of limes but all wuthering in appearance, bleak, & the road a grass track ...... Barns in decay. Then the back of a rather forbidding Farm house, we walked round to the front of it & saw to our amazement in the Blazing SUN a perfect English Country House. But with a view onto Downs before it that took our breathes away. You know the sort of house my grandmother drew in pencil in huge drawing Books. A verandah, grey slate roof and a sloping grass lawn as soft as the most expensive velvet. But from the windows one gazed out onto the most marvellous downs in the world!! The house lay in fields which sloped at a distance of half a mile to the great downs. Only sheep grazed round & a few cows. Not another house could be seen, or a village. Lovely red copper beeches & huge ash trees shaded the lawn. It even possessed an ilex tree in the garden ... It faced south so one would never shiver with the damp & cold as one does here.'[3]

After eight years of loving friendship Carrington and Lytton had reached a point of what the French call 'tendresse', living 'every day in utter and complete intimacy, even if separated'. The atmosphere at Ham Spray was partly born out of this sensibility. Lytton was painfully aware of what he felt to be his lack of physical attractions. But at Ham Spray Carrington created an environment for Lytton where he could be 'a bearded El Greco saint living in an Ilex bower'[4] and as Richard Hughes, author of *A High Wind in Jamaica*, described: 'My first impression was of the extraordinary beauty of the inside of the house – a beauty based on little original architectural distinction ... my general impression, however, was that he looked as if he had been designed as the perfect objet d'art to go with the background of the house.'[5] Carrington would later write to Lytton: 'It seems ridiculous after 10 years to still tell you that I care so much, but every time you go away it comes back to me, and I realize in spite of the beauties of the Ilex tree & the Downs, Ham Spray loses more than half its beauty robbed of its Fakir.'[6]

Gerald wrote that compared to Carrington 'other women seem vulgar and without taste. She has on them the same effect as Dorelia has. She does not make them seem less beautiful, not less intelligent but she deprives them of that intimate connection between beauty and intelligence which is taste.'

By the middle of the 1920s Carrington had found new cronies in Dorelia John and Henry Lamb. Their meeting ground was the Hampshire-Wiltshire borders and they became devoted friends. Dorelia positively shunned Bloomsbury and Fry considered Augustus a talent abused. You would not find any of John's work at Charleston, but his drawings hung at Ham Spray. For those who came to stay Ham Spray was a complete way of life; a haven and refuge; a place of work and festivity; a place of rest but also a place of inspira-

Letter drawing, Ham Spray
House, 22 July 1924

tion. For Carrington it became the most complete green world and a stage upon which she assembled characters. Rosamond Lehmann wrote of her character Anna in *The Weather in the Streets*: 'Anna does love that house. She says one could paint all one's life within a two-mile radius from the door … she lives an intensely concentrated inner life of thought and feeling, but never highbrow, priggish or pedantic … [she is] the most unvulgar woman I've ever known.'[7]

And Carrington really did not have to stray far for her inspiration or for the houses of her friends, writing to Bunny: 'I rode Belle on the Downs on Sunday, & I saw two beautiful Swedish Princesses (they were Twins) with yellow curls, & Fra Angelico faces walking on the Downs with an austere Father. They were so beautiful that I thought of nothing else for the rest of the Day. Life is almost too varied … On Friday I lay in the sun under a large sunshade; on a double bed, with a Pale Pink Fur coverlet with Stephen Tennant, Green lizards ran on the Paths, & Tropical Parrots & African

Letter drawing, c. 1925

birds flew in a aviary. On the table mixed up with lunch were marvellous orchids.'[8]

The farm house had been vacated by Major Huth, who had moved up the way to a newly built mansion, and the 'family' – Carrington now mostly spoke in the collective 'we' – made the move in July of 1924. Ham Spray was a rambling house of many windows. A coin dated 1700 had been found in the well, and the original two-storey, flint-built long wing at the east end was thought to date from this time; it had smallish paned windows and was not terribly light. The main part of the house was Regency and pure Jane Austen, flanked along its whole length by an ironwork verandah with a glass top. The garden was an extension of the house and because the verandah helped bring the inside out there was barely a day in the year, even if it meant mufflers and hats, when a meal was not eaten under its awning.

Carrington set about painting the south-facing front pink and put all her energies into transforming the house. Creatively it was a mammoth undertaking which never ended. When they had been at the Slade Iris Tree had said of Carrington: 'you are like a tin of mixed Biscuits your parents were Huntley, & Palmer' and Iris' words well describe the diversity of Carrington's work; not only on canvas but on wood, ceramics (tiles and teapots), paper, leather, glass and walls.[9] Carrington's painting was always a force and whatever surface it was made on, be it wall painting or for wall hanging, it was positive and constructive.

Carrington wrote to Lytton: 'I now have a great many new plans for furnishing H[am] S[pray]. All hideous furniture is to be sold and there are to be far fewer objects in the rooms.'[10] The little front sitting room and the dining room were both sunny, each had two windows facing onto the verandah, and were either side of the garden door. The walls of the downstairs sitting room were originally painted pale blue printed with gold, made by dipping a cut orange into a saucer of gold paint. George Slater, a local man, later distempered it out by mistake and Carrington replaced it with icy pink. Stripey Omega cretonnes covered the comfortable low armchairs and looked a little ill fitting, like elephants would in pyjamas. Toile de

Roses, c. 1928, oil, ink and silver foil on glass. Private collection

Jouy curtains hung at the windows and pleated marbled-paper lampshades, made hurriedly one Christmas, stayed. Duncan Grant's *Mandolin Player* and *Plaster Head* hung in here.

You could sometimes write your name in the dust but tea trays were never sticky and there was always a jug of flowers and a clean linen cloth on the dining-room table. Above the picture rail was a marbled-paper frieze and on the walls painted 'arsenic' green hung Carrington's own pictures; to

93

Carrington painting at
Ham Spray

either side of the Tidmarsh dresser was Duncan's *Juggler and Tightrope Walker*, and a gift from Gerald of some ornamental iron forks from Spain which Mr Slater's young daughter Phyllis used for making toast over the fire for breakfast. Carrington's painted foliage decorations covered the fireplace inset and surround, and the brick built fireplace was fuelled by the wood from their own sawmill. But in the summer laurel or buddleia replaced cut logs and nights were lit by a small crystal chandelier.

Rush-seated chairs from Spain, painted blue, comfortably mixed with more traditional pieces of furniture like the 'tall solid old French cupboard … shipped to England from Provence … its outside … polished like a horsechestnut, and inside … lined with … calendered chintz patterned in red and white'.[11]

In spite of the creaky wooden floorboards on the stairs, which made such a nice bouncing noise at the top of the house, Carrington's presence was very quiet because she was soft footed like a cat. The bare boards were mopped with fragrant cedar-wood oil, which mingled with the spicey scent of

Letter drawing, 21 May 1929

orange and clove pomanders, and were covered with the wrinkled black and pale cotton runners and rugs brought back from Spain. No one else had them and they were thought most unusual.

The front hall was yellow and the arches in the kitchen passage Giotto blue. At the back of the house was the long games room where they played ping pong and shuttlecock, and listened to the gramophone. John Banting painted a large mural there of a 'pregnant' Ralph with a twin inside. Next door was the room used for arranging flowers and keeping the empty wine bottles (which had been washed out with shot) in preparation for bottling the barrels of wine they brought back from France, and Carrington painted a decoration on the cellar door of 'a vineyard scene, with Boozing youths & a fox contemplating the grapes'.[12]

The floor above was used for their personal bedrooms, the best spare room and Lytton's library, and had wonderfully bucolic views of the downs. Carrington planned the complete furnishing of Lytton's library and her sketchbooks are filled with designs characterized by their Benthamite principle of usefulness-for-purpose: open bureaus showing small drawers and pigeon holes; pilasters and capitals for fitted furniture and, most importantly, shelves for books.

The final designs were classical and elegant, and made by Mr Slater. The bookcases were painted mushroom. At the top was a vignette of an owl resting upon a book, and the cataloguing letters, outlined with elongated octagons, were painted in forget-me-not blue. Between the windows Carrington placed one of her painted panels. The fireplace wall was papered with a hand-blocked design of diamonds within stripes in a dusty pink and yellow and hung with a print by Huber of 'Voltaire blessing us with up-raised hand'.[13] Carrington painted the tiles with sunflowers,

Lytton's library at Ham
Spray c. 1926

Lytton's initials, urns of flowers and crested hoo-poes with ribbon-tail feathers.

Carrington very often made printed papers with potato cuts. She covered Gerald's edition of *Anthony and Cleopatra* with a pattern of fan shapes in green and black. She also covered and labelled some of Lytton's books and made him Italian letter cases out of Bromo boxes for his table. Leading from Lytton's library was a door to a boxroom, which, with Mr Slater's help, Carrington transformed into a *trompe l'œil* bookcase, the shelves corresponding with the others in the room. It was the kind of illusion that Carrington thrilled to. She decorated the projecting spines of the 'books' with realistic bindings of her own making and labelled them all with subterfuge titles: *The Empty Room* by Virginia Woolf, *False Appearances* by Dora Wood, *Deception* by Jane Austen.

When Lytton was away from Ham Spray this was the room where Carrington spent her evenings, among the books, with a log fire burning and Phyllis and Olive for company. Olive was Phyllis' elder sister, and the cook-housekeeper. They made patchwork quilts together, Olive fixing the patches to templates and Carrington sewing them. Carrington encouraged Phyllis to read and selected the novels of Jane Austen for her. Carrington described to Gerald what this activity meant to her: 'Yesterday evening I spent mending my patchwork-counterpane, with more patches. I

95

Bookplate for Lytton,
*c.*1925, woodcut

LYTTON STRACHEY

The bulrushes, on the supports, were black and brown highlighted with blackbird-egg blue. And the two-handled vases, so common in Carrington's own flower paintings, sitting on stoney plinths, were coloured with orange, turquoise, black, mustard and white against a biscuit background. In the photograph (taken after Carrington's death) two small portraits of parrots, one golden, one green, framed in silver wood sit on the mantelpiece.

Most of the guest rooms were in the old part of the house, but the best guest room was opposite Lytton's bedroom, on the north side, and 'the

think it's a strangely romantic occupation – These faded pieces of cotton, twenty, or fifty years ago the print dress of some lovely welsh servant, the frock of a young girl of 15, the pinafore of a little girl of 6, the apron of a plain fat girl in a Baker's shop, the petticoat of Mrs Slater's mother … the purple-flowered drawers of Mrs Slater's niece who died when she was twelve. And even miss moffat's [Carrington's] faded cotton dresses creep in, – & a purple patch from a bed spread from Fitzroy Street.'[14]

The beauty and desirability of patchwork coverlets and quilts is now recognized and it no longer seems far-fetched to compare this art form, made with the dual considerations of practicality and looks, to the collages made by Kurt Schwitters out of scraps of paper and old, pink bus tickets; the components are chosen with a similar feeling and the same spirit informs both.

In 1928 Carrington's first studio became Lytton's bedroom when she moved to the east end of the house to a room, 'like the bows of a ship with 4 windows', which she painted pale blue.[15] She wrote to Lytton that she would make his bedroom one of the most exquisite rooms in England. The wall above the fireplace was sponged and the extravagant pier glass was outlined with a shadow of colour paler than the surrounding wall, like the leaves of a pineapple top.

Carrington's own tiles were later replaced with a mosaic fireplace by Boris Anrep; his subject of an hermaphrodite was clearly a portrait of Carrington and a more appropriate bedroom decoration for Lytton than Adam and Eve had been. The colours Boris used fitted into Carrington's overall scheme.

RIGHT Carrington on the verandah at Ham Spray with Tiberius, *c.*1928

pollarded trunk of the great aspen seen through the window was nearly always chock-full of barn owls'.[16] The walls were painted pink and it had a four-poster bed with green and white posts and yellow curtains, and a paper lantern hanging from the ceiling painted with a canary on a swing in a cage. There was a crewel-work cat and a very large jar of Best Birds Eye Tobacco.

Carrington's own four-poster had bed curtains made from chintzes, sent by Gerald, depicting a Rousseauesque scene of 'two tigers in a jungle on a blue background',[17] which she would slip behind at the end of the day in scarlet silk pyjamas and dressing gown 'speckled like an eastern sky'.[18] And

Carrington wrote to Gerald of her plans for the walls: 'I shall paint all the wood work in my room pale-yellow-green, only so pale, it will be the colour of the calyx of a primrose and on the walls I shall frame, in pale yellow wood frames, my new pictures of birds that Margaret Waley sent me yesterday.'[19]

Phyllis often posed for Carrington: with a tennis racket in her school gingham dress or behind the kitchen window as an eighteenth-century cook. She also sat in the pink room, for which Carrington paid her six pennies, taken from a Victorian silk-netted purse, and gave her the portrait. But when Phyllis grew to the sensitive age, with boy-

Lytton's bedroom at Ham Spray, with Boris Anrep's hermaphrodite fireplace. Photograph taken after Carrington's death

97

Carrington in the field
beyond the haha at Ham
Spray, c. 1928

friends calling, she disliked the image of herself. She could not understand why her neck should be so long, her lips pouty and eyes so disconcertingly blue, and one day she took her father's axe to it.

In June Carrington's dusty hair was bleached in stripes like wheat straw and her eyes looked even more blue in her brown face because of the time she spent out of doors. Come rain, come shine, Carrington was hardly ever out of the garden, in the incongruous garb of print frock and white rubber boots when planting; an old Mackintosh when feeding corn to the fantail pigeons who domiciled above the garage, but who danced quadrilles on the lawn; or in beekeeper's hat under swathes of black netting when attending to the hives in the kitchen garden.

Phyllis also sat with the carter's daughters, Iris, Gladys and Cis, in the tall grass of the meadow at the bottom of the front lawn beyond the haha. She read to them from a picture book and sang 'Just a wee deoch-an-doruis', to keep them entertained while Carrington painted. According to Phyllis, Carrington was pleased with the painting, but it does not seem to have survived and one cannot help but lament its loss as well as others for which there are teasing indications in sketches and illustrations in letters.

Carrington's sketchbooks were her commonplace-books in which she wrote and drew. Leaf upon leaf is covered with rapid notations of thought, sketches of arrested moments and of people engaging with one another, which invite us into the intimacy of the scene. Most of these sketches remained thoughts rather than helps to paintings. In one sketchbook Carrington pictured an intriguing composition of four men in conversation around a table, in the exclusivity of a curtain-hung booth; on another page three Latin men dance before an audience, one stepping over a lighted candle without the flame flickering. Interior life at Ham Spray was captured in eloquently penned conversation pieces such as that of Leonard Woolf and Saxon Sydney-Turner sitting over an intensely considered game of chess, or in a firelit scene, with Lytton on the edge of his chair facing his bear-like companion Boris Anrep, who sits plumply back and listens to what he has to say.

Carrington clearly had a fascination with the

The Gamekeeper's Sons, Tidmarsh, letter drawing, January 1919. 'Yesterday those little boys came & I worked all the afternoon on them, and got on fairly well with it. They are so charming – I quite love their fat shining faces and droll naïve characters.' Harry Ransom Humanities Research Center. The University of Texas at Austin

conquest of light over dark, but whereas she drew it often, she rarely painted night. One such painting, a watercolour of three friends bathing their feet in a circular tub illuminated by the casting glow of a candle, has what Matisse called 'une harmonie d'ensemble'. In it Carrington combined the rhythm and blocked-out colours of Matisse's

Lytton Strachey and Boris Anrep in the front sitting room at Ham Spray, *c.* 1927, pen and ink on paper, 35.6 × 33 (14 × 13). Collection of Charles E. Whaley

The *'Roman Bath'*, *Tidmarsh Mill*, 1919, ink and wash on paper. Private collection

OPPOSITE Study for *The Feetbathers*, 1919, pencil on paper, 25.5 × 21.5 (10 × 8½). Courtesy: Anthony d'Offay Gallery, London

Carrington and Alix Strachey, mid 1920s

paintings of 'The Dance'; the cylinder, sphere and cone of Cézanne's paintings of 'Bathers', and William Blake's linked figures in *Oberon*, *Titania and Puck with Fairies Dancing*. And it is interesting to see how the detailing in the preparatory drawing of the Lolita in quatrocento dress, pulled up to reveal her frilly drawers and lean legs, is erased in the watercolour.

As Carrington's experiences with Gertler, and later with Brenan, had shown, she was divided over her sexuality and was perhaps more Sapphic than not. As she grew older she felt less inhibited about following her inclinations and experienced ecstasy, without shame, with at least one woman: Henrietta Bingham. Henrietta had rather remarkable looks when she was lit up at night and 'the face of a Giotto Madonna. She sang exquisite songs with a mandoline, southern state revivalist nigger songs'[20] and Carrington wrote to Alix Strachey: 'I am very much more taken with Henrietta than I have been with anyone for a long time. I feel now regret at being such a blasted fool in the past, to stifle so many lusts I had in my youth, for various females.'[21]

Carrington made two frankly erotic, sensual drawings of women in the mid 1920s, which are completely winning. In pen and ink, using a very fine nib, like the hardest pencil, Carrington drew Henrietta in a most revealing and unselfconscious stance. The attitude of her right arm is beautifully drawn and the fetishistic addition of shoes makes her nudity nakedness. In a hilarious letter to Julia Strachey Carrington teasingly described how shoes could win her heart: 'Under the excuse of examining the buckles, I gave them a delicate stroke, and the thrill that ran down my spine, my dear! I can hardly describe!'[22]

Julia regularly stayed at Ham Spray and Carrington wrote about the frustrations of one visit to Gerald: '[t]he maddening thing is that I actually have (or rather don't "HAVE") a lily white lady with Chinese eyes & arms of purest milk sleeping night after night in my house, & there's nothing to be done, but to admire her from a distance, & steal distracted kisses under cover of saying goodnight.'[23]

Although she was at one time a model to Poiret in Paris, and slender, Carrington's fantasy pictured

Henrietta Bingham, c. 1923,
pen and ink on paper,
$(26 \times 17\frac{1}{2})$. Collection:
Duke of Devonshire

Julia as 'very fat, and like a Veronese beauty'.[24] A frisson of sexuality, through nakedness adorned, electrifies the drawing. The long rope of pearls wrapped, provocatively, twice around her throat contrasts strangely with Julia's prim little fringe and mouth. Julia is an odalisque and ravishing, with the come-hither body of Goya's *Naked Maya* and the cooler expression of Manet's *Olympia*.

Carrington also sent Julia a drawing of a comely woman with a pussy nestled in her lap; the cat has just twitched its tail and her toes curl with pleasure (see p. 59). In a second version she attached a brassiere of wire and black net that could be operated with a lever to reveal her breasts.

In rather innocent contrast to these two women, Carrington's delightful drawing of the dormouse-like Vivien, Dorelia's younger daughter, is remarkably chaste, particularly considering Lytton described Vivien as 'a most imposing personage – half the size of Poppet and twice as dangerous'.[25]

Vivien posed for Carrington in the 'ghost room' at Fryern Court. Fryern was rather like Ham Spray, except Vivien thought Ham Spray was 'prettier, slightly more organized', and as such Fryern was home from home and a bolt hole for Carrington. It was also 'a haven of fair women and Siamese cats' presided over by Dorelia, Sybil-like, and life there was very much to her taste.[26] After breakfast Carrington and Dorelia's 'ravishing daughters'[27] would sit on Dorelia's bed and talk in a 'mélange of recumbent females', 'like a scene in an African harem', which greatly appealed to Carrington.[28]

Julia Strachey, c. 1925, pencil on paper, 47.7 × 63.5 (18 × 25). Private collection

103

Vivien John, c.1928, pencil, pen and ink on paper, 19.8 × 24.8 (7¾ × 9¼) (present whereabouts unknown)

you can't get James [Strachey, i.e. psychoanalysed] can't you take yourself in hand in some way? Be a little less self-repressive, for instance? & a little more easy going. May I say that it is obvious to everyone that you do far too much & neglect yourself?'[32]

Henry was also Carrington's ally against the mood of the moment for 'isms' and the group system, writing one year at crocus time: 'I thought Roger amusing & picturesque but really he has the bigotry of a common proselyte the observation of a bat & about as much sense of direction & range of flight. And then a comic sort of rectorial suffisance.'[33]

Carrington was as much fascinated with the physical selves of people: their looks, their clothes and the impression they made, as with the emotional sides of their natures, and she rarely missed an opportunity to paint portraits. Carrington persuaded Catharine Alexander, also a painter, to pose one day, in a Victorian button-backed chair, when she was at Ham Spray for lunch.

Catharine was Noel's 'new young lady ... very lovely, a Perugino angel with a wide forehead and golden hair'.[34] Her youthfulness made her a little in awe at Ham Spray, and no doubt privy to this, Carrington painted a touching portrait of vulnerability, capturing all the life and play that light makes on a young girl's complexion. Catharine remembers sitting for her portrait: 'I think we didn't talk much ... she liked to seriously get on with the painting. I think it took three or four sittings. I do remember Ralph creeping into the studio and being shooed out by Carrington as she wanted to quietly get on without a lot of talk.'[35]

As early as 1917, Carrington had written to Lytton about 'the still picture. You know it might be good as I have suddenly discovered a method of putting on the paint & getting what I want.'[36] She may have been referring to *Beeny Dogs* but this confidence and technical skill became very apparent in her portraits.

Carrington could be as critical of others as she was of herself and consequently her portraits were always telling and sometimes unflattering. Carrington painted a portrait of her Slade friend Margaret Waley in January 1921, whose daughter said: 'it was rather savage, my mother could be

Vivien remembers one painting: 'I was just a glum little girl with a nice scarf with beautiful spring flowers in it.' Henry Lamb had written to Carrington that he was impatient to see the Vivien head: 'I envied you staying on with your gift of mesmerizing Vivien & the others into sitting for you.'[29] Vivien found Carrington: 'very vivacious, a great talker, but not aggressively talking ... the first adult I remember to bring one out and get one to talk ... I blossomed under her charming attention and sympathy and became a little dependant on her ... but I don't think she wanted that ... she had a kind of a certain reserve which was quite strange.'[30]

Henry became Carrington's chief confidante and wrote constantly to 'Carissima Carrington' over the next few years. They exchanged gifts of drawings and paintings; Henry gave Carrington angel's tears for her 'rockery place', and they compared notes on plants' progress and the horrors of black, green and brown flies.

Henry, Julia observed, was very much like Carrington. It had something to do with their personal demons and 'the wealth of creative passion that lies within them'.[31] Because of this affinity, Henry was an astute and encouraging critic, and a caring friend who could write to her: 'well, if

Catharine Alexander (later Carrington), *c.* 1924, oil on canvas, 40.6 × 30.5 (16 × 12). Collection: Duke of Devonshire

Olive Slater, 1925, oil on canvas, 44 × 33 (17¼ × 13). John Martin

extremely bad tempered and I think Carrington caught some of this ... it wasn't an appealing side of my mother's nature and therefore, to have it static, looking at one all the time was uncomfortable.'[37] This painting was relegated to a blind spot and then mysteriously disappeared. Others have followed suit.

Gertler thought the teenage daughter of 'the Bussys ... a sort of Lytton Strachey in petticoats!' and so she appears in Carrington's doll-like portrait of her on a chaise longue, looking dignified but down at mouth.[38] Considering it was not her most successful painting, Carrington chose an ambitiously-sized canvas for *Janie* which gives an unprecedented view of the uncluttered space of a Ham Spray room with bare boards and an impressive gilt-framed, floor-to-ceiling mirror.

Keynes described E. M. Forster as 'the elusive colt of a dark horse', and whereas Janie sat for her portrait, Carrington painted a remarkable likeness of Forster without him sitting. The portrait was one of the paintings Henry Lamb referred to when he wrote to Carrington: 'I want very much to see your new portraits & their shiny noses & fore-

heads'[39] and having seen it, wrote again in the most eulogistic terms, best appreciated when one understands that he was a talented musician: 'O, yes: I think there is something so very good about your head of Forster, – I mean it shows a combination of all your best Haydnesque qualities with the true beginnings of the kind of amelioration that is needed to make them all eventually turn into Mozartian masterpieces.'[40] Carrington's achievement lay in capturing both the illumination of Forster's soul and the flood of daylight upon his face.

Lamb generally knew what Carrington was painting, which was an honoured position because not many people did. In 1916 Carrington had written to Gertler 'I would like you to be interested in my work as I am in yours' but she also knew that 'you will never have a passion for another person's point of view and desires, as your own is so great', and until Carrington met Lamb she was deprived of a painter's communication.[41]

In July 1926 Carrington was painting portraits of Julia and Olive; their treatment could not have been more different. In the same chair that Carrington painted the earthy portrait of Catharine, she portrayed Julia as an exquisite. Her dress and turban of silks, the pearly skin-tones and symphony of sweet-pea colours fit the portrait for an Elizabeth Arden advertisement. The seductive gossamer quality of this picture, however, rather belies the expression Carrington captured on Julia's face, which friends knew could mean she was about to be very crushing.

According to Frances Partridge, Julia 'was a very acute, fastidious critic, she admired Carrington no end and was fascinated by her'.[42] Julia wrote of Carrington: 'For me, in my twenties, she produced powders and perfumes, hats, beads and ribbons; she helped dress me up to go out to parties, and entered into all my most fantastic projects for plays or performances.'[43]

Carrington had trunks full of embroideries, silks and brocades, garnered from her travels, in which she dressed her sitters. She herself would have liked to dress in nothing but silk dressing-gowns and shawls. When Noel was in India Carrington had asked him to seek out Kashmir shawls and silk coats 'as worn by Hill Tribemen & Persians', but she was only interested in the old ones.[44] She based her own clothes on them too, writing to Gerald Brenan: 'I cut out my green grass brocade dress … It is a copy of my Persian dress … It's going to be very elaborate, green silk stockings and scarlet shoes and an underdress of fine red silk.'[45]

In contrast, there is no mystery about Carrington's portrait of Olive. She painted a solid picture of a young country girl she came to think the world of. Olive was Annie's successor and only fourteen when she came to Ham Spray in March of 1925, but with a maturity and steadfastness beyond her years. Within no time she was Carrington's 'attendant spirit', lighting the morning fires, baking biscuits and pies, making quince jelly to Mrs Beeton's recipe, and brewing up the vinegar rinse that Carrington used to wash her hair.

What is unusual, for this period, about the portrait (which Carrington gave to Olive) is that Carrington painted Olive as Goya had painted Señora Sabasa García: in a shawl against a very dark background of charcoal green. The inky blue of her simple dress is embellished with one of Carrington's patterned shawls, coloured in ochres and ambers, chosen to complement Olive's Goyaesque colouring and reddish hair.

Carrington had a simple and fundamental understanding with all the Slaters. There was nothing intellectual about it; the pages of Olive's copy of Eminent Victorians, inscribed to her by Lytton, were never cut. George Slater was the church organist, an orthodox man and full of faith. He was also a parish councillor and on polling day one year Carrington helped him to bring in the Liberal vote, wearing a yellow coat and driving her yellow Sunbeam car, decked with yellow ribbons, from eight in the morning to eight at night.

In the late 1920s Carrington also began painting small, fleetingly done, portraits on canvases the size she had once reserved for travelling. Lamb asked about one of these when he wrote, in 1927: 'the head of Ritchie sounds good – is it quite small & done in one sitting like the first one?'[46] Philip Ritchie was Lytton's latest lover whom Carrington did not much like. As his ramrod back and tight expression testify, she found Ritchie 'rather tedious' and suspected 'he must have been very pruddish in his youth'.[47] Carrington did, however,

make a breakthrough painting of him that suggests her handling of paint was changing, and also shows how a portrait can be greater than the sum of its parts. Not only did Carrington create an accurate image of Ritchie as he looked but also, through the skilfull use of paint, managed to convey how he seemed to her.

The method of putting on paint that Carrington evolved in Ritchie's portrait was also used for the landscapes she painted from Ham Spray about this time. All of Carrington's easel energies went into painting the downs swelling up before the house like a blown-out counterpane, because the flat, pink façade of the house did not have the picturesque qualities of Tidmarsh. Lytton had bought Carrington a rough white pony from Mr Coker, the butcher in Hungerford, and through riding Belle daily on

Philip Ritchie, 1927, oil on canvas, 35.5 × 30.5 (14 × 12). Private collection

107

Letter drawing, 24 January 1927: 'The cold is intense, just as I was settling down to paint this morning looking like this blown out with jerseys, overcoats, aprons, socks and fur shoes with a dribbling nose and unbrushed hair …'

the downs, Carrington came to know them as intimately as she had known Sheepless Down and the Netherton Valley by Hurstbourne Tarrant. A letter Carrington wrote to Gerald describes the intimacy of her relations with Lytton and the world she mostly painted from her window: 'I sit up in bed, and watch a curious world on a green stage. The loves of cows, cats hunting rabbits in groves of laurels, gargantuan feasts given by black birds on the lawn, the provincial life of the rooks in Ilex

Cattle by a Pond, c. 1930, oil on canvas, 40.6 × 35.6 (16 × 14). Reproduced by kind permission of Sotheby's

Carrington and Lytton under the weeping ilex tree at Ham Spray

tree and last night the great brown owl padded softly through the sky past my window. The only thing that makes it a pleasure to be ill is the beauty of the room when the fire casts great shadows from my bed across the ceiling and Lytton sits on the little low Spanish chair framed against the black Ilex in the window reading Tamburlaine.'[48]

There are many more references to paintings of the land than surviving pictures. Although Carrington painted fields of ripening corn, the known landscapes are mostly wintry ones, when the cold was intense. Henry Lamb sent 'winter condolences' in January 1926, with his sympathies that 'now the snow is all gone and you will be cussing about your unfinished landscape', which suggests that Carrington was painting directly from nature rather than composing pictures in her studio.[49] It was the way she was painting portraits, with an immediacy, and on a small scale which could be soon finished.

One of the most poignant and evocative of Carrington's landscapes is disarmingly modest (only 12 inches by 14 inches), and has similar spiritual qualities to the interior painted, time and again, by Gwen John of her Paris studio on the rue

Terre Neuve, to the same scale and in the same period. Carrington wrote one January: 'The sun was just setting, and the sky was a most delicate green tinged with pink and little clouds rose up from behind the crest of the downs, like balloons liberated by some hidden hand and floated up into the pale opal sky ... The country intoxicates me with its beauty ... To my mind this landscape is at its loveliest in the winter, covered with snow.'[50]

In the *Downs from Ham Spray in winter* the boles of the two beeches in the foreground grow so closely together they must embrace; they share a shadow which casts them on an island. Behind and to either side they are flanked by two grouped audiences, two isolated stands of beeches, their branches so intertwined they appear feathery at the tops and, beyond that, a whiplash of trees, known locally as the 'Bull's Tail', which defines the crest of Downey Hill.

As with previous pictures, this painting would seem a comment on Carrington's life. The *Downs in winter* breathes rather than pulses and has a resonance quite unlike Carrington's earlier landscapes. Aided by the snow, and like the uncluttering of the house, it has a spatial quality devoid of

On the Sands at Dawlish Warren, c. 1923, oil on canvas, 32.4 × 36.2 (12¼ × 14¼). Private collection

at Dawlish Warren is a lightning study, perhaps painted in one sitting, which stylistically belongs here because it is as unfussed and pregnant a picture as the *Downs from Ham Spray in winter*. And, as in that picture, it is a painting in shorthand. Colour, unusually, is not the most important element and Carrington's palette is restrained, allowing the drama of the situation to do the work.

Carrington had painted on the sands at Dawlish Warren, Devon, on one of the rare occasions when she had joined Ralph in visiting his family at nearby Starcross. The dull light in this picture, of an overcast day in England, reflects the chilly, unconvivial atmosphere of Cofton, the Partridge family home.[51] The brown- and yellow-haired children are hatless out of doors which helps point to the late date. They are the same spidery folk Carrington evolved for her landscapes, seemingly for the sake of the composition, but that is just a ruse because this is also a study of 'the misery of authorized fun'.[52] Two women, one a nun in a floating veil, and eight young girls flock together like sandpipers on the pale yellow strand under a lowering sky as the incoming tide approaches. The linking of hands between the nun and a child is the configuration seen before; the other woman is wielding a stick at a ghostly child – the only one who is thinly painted – who makes a Carel-Weight-type dash for liberty.

There is also a curious echo in this painting of the impressionism of Steer who made several studies of the flat beaches of Suffolk. But what it suggests most of all is that Carrington had developed a mature way of painting and a lightness of touch that captured the essence of her idea.

surplus detail. In a letter to Julia, in January 1927, Carrington described her 'hermitage life' with Lytton at Ham Spray. Ralph now spent a greater part of each week away. In the spring of 1926 Ralph and his new love, Frances Marshall, began living openly together in London. Frances had been educated at Bedales with Julia and had met Ralph in 1922 when he was travelling books for the Hogarth Press and she was working in the Birrell & Garnett bookshop in Bloomsbury.

Carrington often painted the rocks and sea in Cornwall but none of these seascapes seem to have survived. Carrington's small painting, *On the Sands*

8 Vanitas. Fugitive Light

In her last years Carrington's green world offered most of what she desired. Her life became more interior and the subject of her art more minutely attended to. Paradoxically, as Carrington's life found stability and rootedness with Lytton she began to paint some very large portraits of flowers and objects, seemingly chosen and arranged in the vanitas tradition, which served as a reminder of the transience and uncertainty of life.

Carrington had always painted flowers – Lytton had praised the picture of flowers in a pot she exhibited at the NEAC in 1916 – but they now became more prominent. Flowers were painted against pointilist walls; on patterned, plain, or plush cloths. They offered up endless permutations for showing texture and, most importantly of all, colour and light. Like Winifred Nicholson, Carrington never tired of painting flowers. Of all varieties, the naturally selected colours found in dahlias and tulips satisfied her the most, and Carrington painted these blooms over and over again, with different characters and different moods.

In a contemplative picture, gently coloured, of mixed dahlias in a jug, Carrington used the end of her brush to incise the decoration on the terracotta, in much the same way the potter had done. She used the stub of her brush again for raising the pattern in the sunburst yellow centres. It was the first time she had fiddled on canvas with anything other than the bristle end of a brush and brings to mind the punch marks by Sassetta in his tempera paintings on poplar. She then painted the dahlias again, more intensively coloured, in an altogether more strident version on the same slate surface, but this time in a loving cup.

In marked contrast, Carrington's baroque painting of *Tulips in a Staffordshire Jug* is a monumental flowerpiece and one of Carrington's boldest paint-ings made, one imagines, in a frame of mind when she felt powerful and completely sure of her gifts. With its blend of illusionism – it is painted much larger than actual size (the tiny jug can be seen on the top of the Tidmarsh dresser p. 58) – colour and movement it has a direct emotional appeal.

Carrington had grown white parrot tulips in her window box at Gower Street and in the garden at

Dahlias (unfinished), c. 1927, oil on canvas, 60.9 × 50.8 (24 × 20). Private collection

White flowers in two-handled jug, c. 1925, 50.8 × 40.6 (20 × 16). Corporate Art Collection, The Reader's Digest Association Inc.

BELOW RIGHT *Flowering cactus, c. 1931, oil on canvas, 76.7 × 45.7 (30¼ × 18). Private collection*

Tidmarsh, and at Ham Spray she planted an entire bed of different varieties. Carrington wrote of painting tulips throughout her life, but this is perhaps the one referred to in April 1921 which she exhibited at the 'Nameless' exhibition: 'I started a still-life yesterday of tulips, and I was so pleased with it that I stay here alone to finish it.'[1] As in Olive's portrait the inky background has little precedent in her work; the bleeding sunset colours of the curling-tongued tulips and the over-all thickness of the paint suggest that the picture was well worked but that she knew when to stop.

Carrington took a different approach again when she painted a red flowering cactus, perhaps one of the rare cactuses that Dorelia had given her in July 1931 for her hothouse. Such was her eagerness to paint it, she put the pot, still in its tissue paper, into a saucer of water and then placed it on the bare wooden floor against the corner of a blue wall; lightly painting it, by tone, almost twice the size she had been painting portraits.

On one of her forays Carrington found some large blue glass chemists' jars with chemical formulas transferred onto their rounded sides in gold. Carrington had started making jewel-like illumi-nations on glass backed with tinsel, like silver

OPPOSITE *Dahlias, c. 1925, oil on canvas, approx. 61.2 × 45.8 (24 × 18). Private collection*

moons behind lamps, as early as 1923, and there was something alchemical about her own work on glass. Although they have their models, Carrington's style of tinselled pictures appears to be quite unique in England at the time.

Chinese mirror paintings had been imported into England since the eighteenth century and Gains-borough had used painted glass plates to create a sense of recession for the landscapes he composed in his studio. In the nineteenth century 'treacle' pictures were sold for mass consumption. During Victoria's reign 'pearl' paintings on glass, backed with metallic foils to create 'sparkling accents' were a common period pastime, as were the por-traits of actors in heroic guise, dressed up from prints, with assorted fabrics, sequins and embossed foils (Carrington had an example of 'Mr Phelps as Coriolanus').[2]

*Fishing Boat in the
Mediterranean, c.* 1929, oil
on canvas, 35.6 × 33
(14 × 13). Private
collection

HMV gramophone cabinet
commissioned by Alix
Strachey, 1927,
93 × 48.3 × 50.2
(36¾ × 19 × 19¾).
Portsmouth City Museum
and Art Gallery

Julia Strachey, 1925, oil on canvas, 38.1 × 33 (15 × 13). Private collection

The Feetbathers, 1919, watercolour on paper, 43.2 × 35.6 (17 × 14). Private collection

118

The barque Harmony in the ice off the Labrador coast, c. 1929, tinsel painting on glass. Private collection

OPPOSITE *Flowerpiece, c.* 1932, oil, ink and silver foil on glass, 49.5 × 39.5 (19½ × 15½). Bloomsbury Workshop

Carrington's tinselled pictures were in the same tradition as all of these but also hinted at the costume of the pearly kings and queens and the ornamental opulence of the saloon bar. But unlike the parlours and tap rooms which come into their own at night, Carrington's glass paintings belong to the day because electric or even candle light do not bring them alive at all.

Henry Lamb called Carrington's 'glass recreations',[3] 'bright spots' and bought several of them: a 'lovely oiseau'[4] and some 'everlastings', of which he wrote: 'One thing has been thrilling & that is having breakfast every morning with my lovely bunch of immortelles: I don't think I can have told you half their attractions – indeed I doubt, I am certain I didn't know many of them till this week & that is one of the highest merits of a picture – to keep some of it's beauties veiled.'[5]

Carrington's tinselled pictures showed the fascination that reflections and fugitive light held for her, but they were also litmus test indications of her fantasy life and expressive of her hopes and desires, in the Mexican tradition of votive pictures. Although there is no mention of Carrington's feelings about the work of Pierre Bonnard, there is a kinship in their preoccupation with their personal worlds, the glorious potential of colour and the kaleidoscopic role of light. On the wall of his studio in Le Cannet, Bonnard made a small altar to the inspirations of his art. Neatly pinned alongside the work of Picasso, Vermeer, Gauguin, and Ancient Greek sculptors were several carefully smoothed out silver sweet wrappers, each marked with a different impress, each one a glistening reminder of the impulse behind all art, light.

Easel paintings were Carrington's currency but most often as tokens of friendship and as something she gave away. Her glass paintings, however, like her woodcuts and signboards, found a ready market, and she sold them with ease through Mr Pullins' antique shop at Ramsbury, The Little Gallery in Chelsea and the Birrell & Garnett bookshop; she even negotiated with Fortnum & Mason. Selling for between 35s and £2 each, the glass pictures provided a regular income that could pay the bills, and Carrington's demand for silver papers soon outstripped the sweet-eating capacity of her friends. It took about two hours to make a small picture and she found it 'a delightful occupation'.[6]

Carrington always called glass painting her 'winter' work, painting exotic, fantastic scenes of heat and light in the gothic time of the year. Carrington described most of the elements that made up her personal mythology for her illuminations when she wrote: 'Dearest Lytton, Yesterday I went with Brett to the Burlington Fine Arts and saw, what I still even on cool reflection, think the best picture I have ever seen. By Piero di Cosimo – a picture completely of wild animals, and the most beautiful birds, in a landscape of bushes, and a distant sea.'[7] She listed the rest of her lexicon for Alix: 'You will be delighted to hear my ambitious nature … Flowerpiece, boxers, balloons, volcanoes, tight rope dancers, Victorian beauties, soldiers, tropical botanical flowers, birds & fruits, are a few of my subjects. I cater for every taste. Ravishing soldiers in Busbies for the gentlemen, & elegant ladies for the Clive Bells.'[8]

As in folk art, the framing was an integral part of every picture made; mirrors, and bird's-eye-maple frames very often with gold slips, were picked up whenever seen and determined the size of the picture painted. Mostly they were a hand-span wide, although Carrington also used the pocket-sized metal and velvet frames made for the first daguerrotypes, and by 1930 she was painting very sophisticated, tinselled flower pieces as large as 20 inches by 16 inches. The large paintings were quite often mirror images of successful designs transferred from canvas to glass; for example, a tinselled picture for Rosamond Lehmann was the reverse image of Faith Henderson's *Dahlias* (p. 113).

Made by the simple device of back-painting on glass, Carrington outlined her design, with a fine nib, in Prussian blue or black ink and filled in with a mixture of translucent and opaque paints. Then, to great effect, just as in his later years Matisse used cut-outs of coloured papers as a complete substitute for painting, Carrington dressed the forms she had painted with a collage of silver papers, stuck directly onto the glass. She almost always used the silver side – the actual colours for the picture came from the painting – but very occasionally we get a glimpse of Terry's All-Gold, and the art was in knowing how much glass to

leave uncovered and how much work the silver papers should do.

For Dorelia John Carrington made two paintings on glass which are good examples of the successful balance between painting and tinselling. In a portrait of a *Spanish Woman*, hot and sensual with beaujolais reds, papers smoothed out like silver leaf are used for the buildings of the white hill town, the woman's face and plump arm; crumpled foil stands away from the glass creating a plush effect for the tableau curtains; a diamond impressed paper is intricately cut and laid to suggest the folds of the scarf, and each flower centre has a differently tooled pattern of circles, ranging from the prick of a pin to the fine end of a brush.

In the second picture, a botanically observed lily before a miniature Hokusai landscape in cool blues, the lily thrusts up on a single fragile polished stem, the petals have a faceted impress and the stamen are fuzzy with pollen, and in contrast to the translucent painting of the flower, an opaque emulsion of blue is laid for the huge expanse of the sky.

Carrington also took tinselling commissions which had a functional application. There were obvious parallels between Anrep's mosaics, made with glass tesserae, and Carrington's own work, and Carrington made four hatch doors for Boris' house at 4 Pond Street, Hampstead, using mirror glass; scratching away the silvered areas and filling them with birds and flowers. Carrington tinselled a glass door for Margaret Waley's house at 51 Ladbroke Grove, choosing an exaggeratedly baroque patterning of tulips in burgundys and blues that would have suited a saloon bar, and her success excited her: 'I enjoyed London, the pleasure of bringing off my door panels so well, raised my spirits.'[9]

For Barbara Bagenal she painted a lute player, and a silvery 'Audubon' owl with the missive 'Time and Tide Wait for No Man'; Julia Strachey had a scene from the Garden of Eden, and for Faith Henderson she painted a Heath Robinson style hot-air balloon floating above a land of cactuses and palms which may have been made from a print in the same way as 'treacle' pictures.

Carrington made a small picture of Iris Tree galloping on a white horse against a midnight sky,

looking like a Joan of Arc with spurs on her heels, a sword belt and sheath, and a billowing blue cloak. This fragile picture became a kind of St Christopher for Iris which she carried with her, and in the 1950s when she was staying in a one-room apartment in Rome 'her little equestrian portrait by Carrington rested against a pile of books on the table'.[10] Carrington also captured 'a very clever and extraordinary likeness' of Frances Penrose.[11]

In the autumn of 1928 Carrington met Bernard Penrose, a hale and hearty yet taciturn young man, who became her last lover. Carrington had found she was incapable 'of sustaining a lover-relation' with Gerald.[12] In the winter of 1927 she wrote to him: 'you will never know the whole of my life. Every time you put me under inquisitions and cross

Lily, c. 1928, oil, ink and silver foil on glass, 30.5 × 25.5 (12 × 10). Courtesy: Anthony d'Offay Gallery, London

OPPOSITE *Spanish Woman*, c. 1928, oil, ink and silver foil on glass, 30.5 × 15.5 (12 × 10). Private collection

One of two panels for an interior door at Margaret Waley's house in Ladbroke Grove, WII, 1927, oil, ink and silver foil on glass

questionings I feel you are trying to separate me from myself. Pulling the bark off my tree ... of all characteristics in human[s] I dread jealousy and possessiveness most.'[13] Gerald had 'perhaps said and felt rather more than is compatible with being friends'.[14]

Beakus, as he was nicknamed, was one of the four Penrose brothers and had broken completely with type and background by going to sea; it was one of the reasons why he became romantically mixed up in Carrington's imagination with her brother Teddie. Teddie died on the Somme in 1916 but he had served on a minesweeper and Carrington preferred to believe he had been lost at sea. With Beakus Carrington could satisfy her 'Shelley craving to sail, & leave these quiet rural scenes for Greek islands'.[15] He had a blue brig tattooed on his forearm; had 'sailed halfway around the world before the mast through storm, salt-lashing seas and scirocco'; had witnessed the staggering beauty of St Elmo's fire and the pampero; considered himself a horny-handed sailor and proud of it.[16]

Beakus was also rather remote, a characteristic which allowed Carrington to experience with him some of the most unadulterated pleasure she had ever known, on his Brixham trawler which he moored at Falmouth. The Sans Pareil was 'an infinitely romantic ship, with brown varnished cupboards and cut glass handles and a little fire place with a brass mantelpiece'; the interior she describes makes it sound like a beautifully crafted gypsy caravan.[17]

Carrington made four touchingly evocative illuminations for Beakus, inspired by his tales of adventures at sea. One of these was of the barque Harmony, the Moravian Mission's 'rum and bible' ship, running gallantly through a deadly obstacle course of icebergs and needle rocks overhung by the sheer black cliffs of the Labrador coast.

Two other pictures feature sailing ships on halcyon seas in tropical paradises with palm trees and, in one, a siren proclaiming 'Bon Voyage'. The third, no doubt, is a stretch of the coastline Carrington and Beakus knew, and has the Sans Pareil sailing on a sea, crested with foam, within sight of unmistakably English chalk cliffs.

Carrington's relationship with Beakus was a protracted one. He always had other girlfriends,

S.V. Sans Pareil, c. 1929, oil, ink and silver foil on glass. Private collection

Bon Voyage, c. 1929, tinsel painting on glass. Private collection

which suited Carrington, but by midsummer of 1930 she quipped to Julia: 'to tell you the Truth when the Gull said ages ago "I wish you'd wear black silk stockings, or dark brown, they show off a leg, so much better than those awful white ones you always wear", I realised our PATHS lay differently.'[18] Beakus was ten years younger than Carrington and did not appreciate the qualities that set her apart. But like Iris, Beakus took his four ships' likenesses with him whenever he moved.

Carrington undertook a great many complete schemes of decoration for the homes of her friends and although she sometimes lamented this diversion from 'serious' painting she embarked upon each new scheme with gusto. Carrington wrote to Dorelia in February 1928 of her plans for a 'Hideous gothic room in King's, belonging to a sweet canary Don called Rylands'. Carrington and Lytton were reading a new novel by Norman Douglas at the time, which, she told Dorelia, was 'rather Greek, and very lecherous', which may account for

the 'Hideous Gothic pictures of roman emperor heads, and Greek urns' which she chose 'to make a nice job of it'.

George Rylands, Dadie to his friends, had become a Junior Fellow of King's College, Cambridge in 1927 and was given (as a temporary measure because the building was scheduled for demolition) a grand set of rooms usually reserved for Senior Fellows. To brighten up the bleak north-facing room Carrington used colours inspired by Dadie's collection of Crown Derby china and he was thrilled from the first. Having previously taken the measurements and made stencils of her designs, Carrington moved in and had completed the scheme in forty-eight hours.

Sponges and brushes (both ends) were used for applying paint, on top of which she intagliated an erratic spiral pattern in the wet paint. The walls were painted pale green. The door jambs were burnt orange flanked on the outside with charcoal blue and dove grey and on the inside with dove

Part of Carrington's decorative scheme for Dr George Rylands' room at King's College, Cambridge, 1928

grey and willow green. The intersections of the doors were painted stone; the panels were bordered with charcoal and dull red and the designs were punched through the stencils in charcoal and orange. As well as four doors, Carrington painted the wooden fireplace surround, and the existing tiles with drapes and bows, Dadie's initials, a compass and rule, feather and open book, trumpets and horns.

For a while Carrington became a roving, jobbing painter, travelling the Wiltshire-Hampshire borders working on the houses of her friends. Carrington found a cottage overlooking the Roman camp on Walbury Hill for Faith Henderson, and then in June 1927 proceeded to decorate it, working meticulously from squared-up sketches. A horn of plenty was painted above one fireplace, using a criss-cross pattern in goldfish colours, with oranges and lemons tumbling out onto a pale blue background. And a bowl-shaped pottery vase of mixed yellow and red dahlias, with green leaves against a dark blue ground, was painted in the sitting room. The walls of the cottage were immensely thick, and in Faith's bedroom Carrington painted orange peacocks on mauve doors edged with 9-inch deep jambs which she painted green with entwining vines.

One very cold winter, Carrington painted Dorelia's little room, lined with cupboards and drawers, plodding on bravely for days on end. The walls were painted with beavers and each one of the twelve drawers was beautifully labelled in ox-blood writing in a painted grey ribbon on a dusty pink ground. Alongside drawers suggesting the collected merchandise of a haberdasher's and a stationer's were Carrington's jokes about Dodo's preoccupations, which meant she need never lose a pair of scissors or be in want of 'rags and bones', 'cats and kittens' again.

For Julia and Stephen Tomlin's house at Swallowcliffe Carrington painted *La Source*, 'a goddess lying by the water's brink, over the sitting room door'.[19] And for the Lambs' house at Coombe Bissett she painted a picture over a door.

Carrington also made contributions to the London houses of most of her friends. For Gerald Brenan's rooms at 14 Great James Street she painted the panelling apple green and vermilion.

Dorelia 'Dodo' John's drawers at Fryern Court, 1928

Dorelia John at Fryern Court, late 1920s

The Cook and the Cat,
tromp l'oeil window at
Biddesden House, 1931

For Lytton's *pied-à-terre* in Gordon Square she was much more chaste, painting the sitting room 'pale green, white and cherry red, with decorations on the mantelpiece'.[20] She decorated Alix's walls, Helen Anrep's 'subterranean refectory' and in July 1930 she wrote to Sebastian Sprott: 'Next week I go to London to draw designs for Phyllis de Janzé's library. She says "I hope it will lead to great things for you." So do I.'[21]

But it would be wrong to suggest that Carrington was painting nothing other than pictures on glass or walls in this period. In the same parcel that she sent Henry Lamb an illumination of a lachenalia, she enclosed a 'Giotto' she had painted in tempera. He was appreciatively grateful, writing: 'it seems to me a divine thing & in spite of all your sneers it continues to give me much more pleasure than I got from any of the originals, ... It has none of the bleakness of most old tempera pictures & all new ones. Also the imagination which contrived that procession of colours is in itself heavenly & that is the part which I will always affirm to be superior to Giotto. Oh I have not had such delight from a picture for ages!'[22]

And in 1931 Carrington painted a *trompe l'oeil* picture on the west front of the Vanbrugh-Hawks-moor style house that belonged to Bryan and Diana Guinness. Phyllis Slater posed for the ghostly cook peeling apples, and Lytton's favourite, Tiberius, sat for the canary-fixated cat. There was something stoical in Carrington's nature; she risked chilblains painting Dodo's drawers on her knees, and a bad cold for the Guinnesses because 'the moment I started to paint it came on to rain. So all my paints got mixed with water. My hair dripped into my eyes and my feet became icy cold. Diana was delighted. Bryan kept it a complete surprise from her till 3 o'ck.'[23]

After finishing the painting, on one of the rare occasions when Carrington asked for an opinion of her work, she wrote to Julia: 'Is the "cook and the pussy cat" an improvement? If you'd tell me that, I should then know whether to go on with my painting, or take to poker-work. But nobody speaks the truth. So it's all no use.'[24] But she later wrote in her diary that she thought she had brought it off and she was glad that Lytton had seen it and liked it.

A little box made by Carrington encapsulates the essence of Carrington's taste and her love of the theatre. The box is covered with shells and lined with fuschia-pink paper, finely spotted with silver and gold. There is a silvered glass in the lid which doubles the pleasure of the inside of the box and also reflects back the moving world within its perimeters.

For Julia 'Carrington was by nature a lover of marvels, a searcher for the emotionally magnificent life; at heart and by vocation she was an impresario, collecting people and their climates, arranging for their exhibition; going to endless trouble in assembling the right properties and accompaniments so that they might display their magic ... in some darkened auditorium out of sight.'[25] Julia repeatedly referred to Carrington in these terms; she saw her as a 'productive creator'. And indeed Carrington loved to produce dramas,

Flowers and drapes, mid 1920s, tinsel painting on glass. Private collection

129

Rachel MacCarthy as 'Daisy' in the film *Dr Turner's Mental Home*, 18 August 1929

whether they be actual performances, or in scaled-down toy theatres for her own amusement – like the clockwork toy of a Dancing Trinity (a gift from Gerald in 1927) which she delighted in dressing with 'pale blue curtains very artificially made & a pink background of flowered wallpaper. The figures look lovely in their new silver paper dresses.'[26]

Carrington's fascination with performance showed itself in her painting. A visitor to Rookfield, where Carrington's overmantel picture for Marjorie Strachey hung, said it reminded him of the third act of *Figaro*, and in 1925 she painted the costumes for the staging of Lytton's first play, *The Son of Heaven* at the Scala theatre in London. She also drew up a scenario, with pictures, for a ballet which she wanted to see performed. She sent the idea to Stephen Tomlin, writing: 'The dairymaids would be dressed in my favourite rustic china-figure-1840-style. You would have to make my masks and help with the inventions, please.' A

seed for the thought had come from Christina Rossetti's poem 'Goblin Market' and, as a tail note to this letter, Carrington wrote: 'The moral I confess of this ballet seems a little obscure. The triumph of Lesbianism?'[27]

Carrington's joke was more than a jest. In 1928 she had written to Sebastian Sprott: 'I still love my horse more than any man, but less than some women' and her diary during the 1930s was full of stories where day time and night time fantasies mingled.[28] The plots were often vividly erotic with arousals, seductions and conquests of women and young girls, and far more potently sexual than any physical encounter Carrington had described with a man.

One weekend in August in 1929 elaborate plans were set afoot for making a film called *Dr Turner's Mental Home*. Beakus had turned up with his cinecamera and the story was based upon a wicked doctor who experimented on the inmates of his mental home, reducing them to animals. Saxon Sydney-Turner played the doctor; Rachel Mac-Carthy played the heroine, 'a simple girl called Daisy' who got drowned in the bath by the greenhouse, and everyone else played the lunatics with Frances excelling as a 'human quadruped lunatic wearing riding boots on her arms'.[29] Carrington's enthusiasm for the project was infectious, but none went as far as joining her at 7 o'clock on Sunday morning and the following Monday making dummies and masks and finding properties for the cast. When the film was shown the following Thursday at 41 Gordon Square it was a big success; Bunny recalled that Saxon wore an expression of such malice as he peered around the door at the luckless Daisy; the film had a 'macabre quality' he had never witnessed before.[30]

Like Chekhov's little bird who was asked why his songs were so short, Carrington had a great many songs to sing and wanted to sing them all.

Conclusion
Time and Tide Wait for No Man

On Thursday, 21 January 1932, in the small hours of the morning when the living often see no hope and the dying are most likely to die, Carrington made the first attempt upon her life. She tried to asphyxiate herself in her car, but Ralph discovered her before it was too late. Lytton died a few hours later, from an undiagnosed and inoperable stomach cancer, after months of anxiety.

Even though Carrington was only thirty-eight, Lytton's death came at a time when she could not imagine creating her life anew; she had lost the ability to be watchful or careful of her self, and her own work offered her no companionship. She was also in the perhaps unusual position of feeling that she had already had the happiest days of her life.

In many ways it appears preordained that Carrington would not reach old age. As early as 1920, on one of the extremely rare occasions when she alluded to the work of women painters as opposed to women writers, Carrington had written to Gerald Brenan how difficult she thought it was to be a 'female creator': 'the few that did become artists, I think you will admit, were never married, or had children. Emily Brontë & her sisters, Jane Austen, Sappho. Lady Hester Stanhope. Queen Elizabeth, and even lesser people like the French female artists Berthe Morrissot, Le Brun, Julie de Lespinasse & Dudeffand ... If when I am 38, I am not an artist, & think it is no good my persevering with my painting, I might have a child.' She married Ralph Partridge against her better judgement a year after this letter, but in 1929 when she was thirty-six and pregnant by Beakus Penrose she had an abortion.

Three years later Carrington wrote to Gerald in a similar vein: 'I often hope I shall die at forty, I could not bear the ignominy of becoming a stout boring elderly lady with a hobby of sketching in watercolours.' And in 1928 she expressed her fears in her diary: 'as one grows older there is no doubt one becomes more particular – fastidious. query. If one becomes *detached* there seems a danger of becoming eccentric, & old maidish, a dislike against the mélange of living too closely against other people.'

In a pen portrait written after Carrington's death, Julia Strachey described Carrington as she knew her in her thirties, calling it 'A Study of a Modern Witch': 'She was a changeling ... From a distance she looked a young creature ... but if one came closer ... one saw age scored around her eyes – and something, surely, a bit worse than that – a sort of illness, bodily or mental, which sat so oddly on so unspoilt a little face, with its healthy pear-blossom complexion.' Julia also knew that Carrington had 'for long spiritually existed

Carrington, Henry Lamb, c. 1926, pencil on paper, 35.9 × 25.6 (14 × 10). Collection of Charles E. Whaley

in the very teeth of some sort of whirlwind, too near whose path she had chanced to stray, and in whose arms, ice-pinnacled and wuthering, she had built her own nest, living there always in readiness, any instant, to cast herself over the edge altogether and to be done with it all.'

Lytton was cremated and his brother James took the ashes which Carrington had wanted to bury under the ilex tree. Lytton had always been Carrington's 'moon' and when he died Carrington's own lights went out. Carrington visited Rosamond Lehmann the day before she killed herself, and Rosamond noticed her euphoria which, with hindsight, was the calm accompanying transcendant mental clarity that came with knowing the end of her suffering was in sight.

Despite every effort of her friends to deflect her from her purpose Carrington made a second attempt upon her life on Friday, 11 March 1932, and

After a picnic at Biddesden House, March 1932 (l to r): Pamela Mitford, Ralph Partridge, Carrington, David Garnett, Frances Marshall

succeeded. Wearing Lytton's purple dressing gown, instead of her own yellow one, Carrington shot herself in her bedroom with a gun she had ostensibly borrowed to kill rabbits. Mrs Waters, the carter's wife, made Carrington comfortable at the end; she said that Carrington hoped and prayed she would live long enough to see Ralph one last time and she died not long after he arrived from London.

In 1930, after particularly frustrating domestic crises which kept her from her painting, Carrington wrote: 'I long for the wings of an owl that I might FLY.' Without her soul mate she felt the only option open to her was oblivion, and in so choosing she liberated herself from the body in which she had always found it so difficult to live.

Carrington was cremated but no one who was there can remember what became of her ashes; and so she lived and died covering her tracks, but failing to obliterate her own tragedy. Although she had the makings of a great painter, Carrington was too gently made and seemingly had no desire for posterity through progeny or paint.

Notes

The following abbreviations have been used:

BL: British Library

Carrington: Noel Carrington (ed.), *Carrington: Paintings, Drawings and Decorations* (London, Thames & Hudson, 1980)

Garnett: *Carrington: Letters and Extracts from her Diaries*, chosen and with an introduction by David Garnett (London, Jonathan Cape, 1970)

Gertler: Noel Carrington (ed.), *Mark Gertler: Selected Letters* (London, Rupert Hart-Davis, 1965)

Gerzina: Gretchen Gerzina, *Carrington: A Life of Dora Carrington 1893–1932* (London, John Murray, 1989)

Julia: *Julia: A Portrait of Julia Strachey by Herself and Frances Partridge* (London, Victor Gollancz, 1983)

Texas: Harry Ransom Humanities Research Center, The University of Texas at Austin

TGA: Tate Gallery Archive

Chapter 1

1 Carrington, p. 20
2 Carrington to Lytton Strachey, 23 September 1926, in Garnett, p. 341
3 This had happened in the previous generation: Ida Nettleship married Augustus John, Gwen Salmond married Matthew Smith, Edna Waugh married Clarke Hall and Stella Bowen married Ford Madox Ford
4 C.R.W. Nevinson to Carrington, 9 September 1912, quoted in Gerzina, p. 42
5 Carrington would have been eager to move on, but her first prize for Painting from the Cast at the end of her third year suggests that she also returned to it
6 Paul Nash, *Outline* (London, Columbus Books, 1988), p. 104
7 Carrington, p. 18
8 ibid., p. 21
9 ibid., p. 15
10 Carrington to Mark Gertler, January 1919, in Garnett, p. 123
11 Nash, *Outline*, p. 162

12 'Mark Gertler: The Man and his Art', *The Studio*, September 1932
13 C.R.W. Nevinson to Carrington, 28 March 1912, quoted in Gerzina, pp. 31–2
14 Mark Gertler to Carrington, February 1915, in *Gertler*, p. 83
15 Edward Marsh to Rupert Brooke, 26 August 1913, quoted in *An Honest Patron: A Tribute to Sir Edward Marsh* (Liverpool, Bluecoat Gallery, 1976), p. 26
16 Edward Marsh to Michael Sadleir, autumn 1913, ibid., p. 26
17 Mark Gertler to Carrington, 14 December 1919, in *Gertler*, p. 177
18 Mark Gertler to Carrington, January 1915, ibid., p. 81
19 Carrington to Mark Gertler, spring 1917, ibid., footnote, p. 144
20 Carrington to Noel Carrington, c. 1918, Carrington, p. 25
21 It was an open competition and all of the 273 students registered that year could apply
22 Mark Gertler to Carrington, July 1914, in *Gertler*, p. 71
23 Carrington to John Nash, n.d. (1913), TGA
24 Carrington to John Nash, n.d. (1913), ibid.
25 Carrington to John Nash, 2 August 1913, ibid.
26 Carrington to John Nash, n.d. (1913), ibid.
27 Carrington to John Nash, n.d. (1913), ibid.
28 Carrington to Gerald Brenan, 6 June 1925, in Garnett, p. 320
29 John Nash to Carrington, n.d. (c. 1914), TGA
30 When Carrington was almost completely forgotten as an artist John Nash sometimes received the credit for her work (Ashridge frescoes and *Hill in Snow at Hurstbourne Tarrant*) and for having influenced her. They shared the very particular sensibilities of the English pastoral tradition and, partly because of this, it has entered the textbooks that Carrington followed Nash, when chronology shows she preceded him.
In 1913, when Carrington was painting her fresco, she had three years of art school training behind her; Nash was completely untrained as an artist and was still working as a journalist on the *Middlesex and Buckingham Advertiser*. Nash, who met Carrington through his brother Paul, visited Carrington at Ashridge and while there made a coloured drawing of the same view that Carrington was painting (Sir John Rothenstein, *John Nash* (London, Macdonald & Co. 1983), illus. p.

14). Nash's *Allotment* is the naive effort of a careful, inexperienced painter. Carrington's own expertise in comparison is obvious, as is her sense of colour, which often surpassed that of Nash. Further comparisons can be made between Nash's *Lloyd George in Hell* (illus. p. 11, ibid.) and Carrington's *Dante's Inferno*.
Nash is also said to have influenced Carrington in the painting of watercolours and the making of woodcuts. For Carrington, however, watercolours were mostly a preparation for oil painting, and Carrington began making woodcuts in 1916, providing illustrations for her first book in 1917, whereas Nash is not known for his cuts until 1919.

Chapter 2

1 Carrington, p. 16
2 Carrington to Barbara Bagenal, 1917, in Garnett, p. 72. Crosse & Blackwell had their pickle-bottling factory at the top of Charing Cross Road
3 Carrington to Gerald Brenan, 12 January 1920, ibid., p. 151
4 *Colour*, 2:2 (March 1915)
5 Carrington to Mark Gertler, n.d., Texas
6 Carrington to Mark Gertler, 1915, ibid.
7 Carrington to Mark Gertler, November 1917, in Garnett, p. 84
8 Frances Spalding, *Vanessa Bell* (London, Weidenfeld and Nicolson, 1983), p. 131
9 Carrington to Mark Gertler, 1917, Texas
10 Carrington to Mark Gertler, December 1916, in Garnett, p. 51
11 Carrington to Mark Gertler, May 1915, ibid., p. 19
12 Carrington to Lytton Strachey, 16 December 1916, BL
13 Carrington to Christine Kühlenthal, n.d. (c. 1914), TGA
14 Carrington to Mark Gertler, n.d. (c. 1916), Texas
15 Carrington to Mark Gertler, December 1916, in Garnett, p. 51
16 'Carrington: A Study of a Modern Witch', in *Julia*, p. 119
17 See Titian, *Portrait of a Man*, 1512 and Baldovinetti, *Portrait of a Lady in Yellow*, both in the National Gallery, London
18 Carrington, p. 20
19 Carrington to Mark Gertler, January 1919, in Garnett, p. 123
20 Carrington to Lytton Strachey, 1 January 1919, ibid., p. 122
21 Carrington to Gerald Brenan, 1 June 1923, in Garnett, p. 253
22 Sacheverell Sitwell, quoted in Carrington, p. 48

23 Carrington's Diary, February 1932, in Garnett, p. 491

24 Carrington to Gerald Brenan, 12 January 1920, in Garnett, p. 152

25 Lytton Strachey to Carrington, 7 July 1918, quoted in Gerzina, p. 134

26 Quentin Bell and Angelica Garnett, *Vanessa Bell's Family Album* (London, Jill Norman & Hobhouse, 1981), p. 31

27 Carrington to Barbara Bagenal, 1915, quoted in Michael Holroyd, *Lytton Strachey: A Biography* (Harmondsworth, Penguin Books, 1971), p. 634

28 Lytton Strachey to Maynard Keynes, 29 August 1916, in Garnett, p. 37

29 Carrington to Lytton Strachey, 10 August 1917, ibid., p. 80

30 Lytton Strachey to Carrington, 23 March 1917, ibid., p. 62

31 Virginia Woolf to Vanessa Bell, 17 January 1918, Nigel Nicolson and Joanne Trautmann (eds), *The Letters of Virginia Woolf*, vol. 2. (London, The Hogarth Press, 1982), p. 212

32 'D. C. Partride [sic] Her Book', 1932, BL

33 Carrington to Gerald Brenan, 15 December 1919, in Garnett, p. 149

34 Carrington to Gerald Brenan, June 1922, ibid., p. 215

35 Virginia Woolf to Carrington, 18 January 1932, *The Letters of Virginia Woolf*, vol. 5, p. 7

36 Virginia Woolf to Carrington, Christmas Day 1922, *The Letters of Virginia Woolf*, vol. 2, p. 596

37 Carrington to Lytton Strachey, 9 August 1930, in Garnett, p. 449

38 Gerald Brenan to Carrington, quoted in Holroyd, *Lytton Strachey*, p. 693

39 Rosamond Lehmann, *The Weather in the Streets* (London, Virago, 1981), p. 264 (first published by William Collins, 1936)

40 Carrington to Lytton Strachey, 13 July 1921, in Garnett, p. 186

41 Carrington to Gerald Brenan, 20 December 1922, ibid., p. 237

42 Carrington to Lytton Strachey, 15 February 1922, ibid., p. 202

43 Carrington to Gerald Brenan, 31 May 1923, ibid., p. 251

Chapter 3

1 Carrington to Lytton Strachey, 30 July 1916, in Garnett, p. 33

2 Carrington to Mark Gertler, September 1916, Texas

3 Lytton Strachey to Carrington, n.d. (1916), BL

4 Aldous Huxley to Frances Peterson, 7 August 1916, quoted in Sybille Bedford, *Aldous Huxley: A Biography*, vol. 1 1894–1939 (London, Chatto and Windus, 1973), p. 69

5 Aldous Huxley, *Crome Yellow* (Harmondsworth, Penguin Books, 1964), p. 15

6 David Garnett, *The Flowers of the Forest* (London, Chatto and Windus, 1955), p. 111

7 Carrington to Lytton Strachey, 5 August 1916, in Garnett, p. 35

8 Mark Gertler to W. J. Turner, 4 January 1923, in *Gertler*, p. 209

9 Carrington to Lytton Strachey, 29 August 1919, in Garnett, p. 143

10 Carrington to Mark Gertler, n.d., Texas

11 Virginia Woolf to Carrington, 15 June 1919, *The Letters of Virginia Woolf*, vol. 2, p. 367. This was a snowscape which, Carrington wrote to Lytton (13 September 1920, BL), was 'incomplete & uninteresting'

12 Virginia Woolf to Carrington, 11 August 1918, ibid., p. 267

13 Carrington to Lytton Strachey, 19 November 1918, in Garnett, p. 118

14 Michael Holroyd, *Augustus John* (Harmondsworth, Penguin Books, 1976), appendix 4

15 Beatrice Elvery, Lady Glenavy, *Today We Will Only Gossip* (London, Constable, 1964), p. 85

16 Carrington to Mark Gertler, n.d., Texas

17 Carrington to Lytton Strachey, 19 December 1916, BL

18 Carrington to Lytton Strachey, 2 April 1917, ibid.

19 Carrington's Diary, 20 March 1931, in Garnett, p. 460

20 Anne Olivier Bell (ed.), *The Diary of Virginia Woolf*, vol. 1 (London, The Hogarth Press, 1977), p. 184

21 Lytton Strachey to Carrington, 31 July 1917, BL

22 Carrington to Virginia Woolf, October 1918, in Garnett, p. 106

23 Carrington to Mark Gertler, January 1919, Texas

Chapter 4

1 Lytton Strachey to Carrington, 6 March 1917, BL

2 George Sampson, *The Concise Cambridge History of English Literature* (Cambridge University Press, 1941), p. 1040

3 Carrington to Noel, 15 July 1921, in Garnett, p. 188

4 Carrington to Lytton Strachey, 20 October 1917, ibid., p. 83

5 Noel Carrington, 'Carrington's Early Life', ibid., p. 504

6 Lytton Strachey to Virginia Woolf, 21 December 1917, Leonard Woolf and James Strachey (eds), *Virginia Woolf & Lytton Strachey: Letters* (London, The Hogarth Press, 1956), p. 66

7 Carrington to Lytton Strachey, 9 November 1917, in Garnett, p. 88

8 Carrington to Lytton Strachey, 18 November 1917, ibid., p. 90

9 Carrington to Lytton Strachey, 18 June 1919, ibid., p. 138

10 Carrington to Lytton Strachey, 20 January 1918, ibid., p. 95

11 Carrington to Lytton Strachey, 19 June 1916, ibid., p. 30

12 Daisy Ashford, *The Young Visiters* (London, Chatto and Windus, 1919)

13 Carrington to Lytton Strachey, 13 July 1921, in Garnett, p. 186

14 Carrington to Lytton Strachey, 29 April 1922, ibid., p. 210

15 Carrington to Lytton Strachey, 1 January 1919, ibid., p. 121

16 Carrington to Gerald Brenan, 18 December 1921, ibid., p. 200

17 Carrington to Gerald Brenan, 3 February 1924, ibid., p. 282

18 Carrington to Gerald Brenan, 31 May 1923, ibid., p. 251

19 Carrington to Lytton Strachey, 11 December 1919, ibid., p. 147

20 Carrington to Lytton Strachey, 15 November 1918, ibid., p. 114

21 Carrington to Gerald Brenan, 16 March 1927, Texas

22 Carrington to Lytton Strachey, 21 May 1919, in Garnett, p. 136

23 Carrington to David Garnett, 26 October 1922, ibid., p. 233

24 Carrington to Gerald Brenan, 20 December 1922, ibid., p. 237

25 Roger Fry exhibited drawings by children from Dudley High School at the Omega Workshops in 1917 and 1919. Carrington wrote to Lytton: 'There is an amazing show of childrens work at the omega. I see proffessional artists are already a thing of the past.' n.d. (c. 1917), BL

26 Jonathan Gathorne-Hardy, *The Interior Castle: A Life of Gerald Brenan* (London, Sinclair-Stevenson, 1992), p. 134

27 Carrington's Diary, February 1932, in Garnett, p. 496

28 Carrington to Mark Gertler, after Christmas 1917, ibid., p. 94

29 'Bloomsbury Group Survivor', *Observer*, 5 March 1972

30 Carrington to Lytton Strachey, 29 April 1922, in Garnett, p. 210

31 Mark Gertler to Carrington, 14 March 1921, in *Gertler*, p. 199

32 Mark Gertler to Carrington, 1 January 1921, ibid., p. 194

33 Carrington's Diary, 14 February 1919, in Garnett, p. 129

34 Gathorne-Hardy, *The Interior Castle*, p. 199

35 Carrington to Lytton Strachey, 14 November 1918, in Garnett, p. 112

36 Carrington to Lytton Strachey, 14 July 1919, ibid., p. 139

37 Carrington to Lytton Strachey, 15 August 1917, BL

38 Carrington to Lytton Strachey, 24 November 1920, in Garnett, p. 170

39 ibid.

40 Carrington to Alix Strachey, n.d. (1920), BL

41 Mark Gertler to Carrington, 26 November 1920, in *Gertler*, p. 187

42 Lytton Strachey to Carrington, 22 July 1920, quoted in Gerzina, p. 162

43 Gerald Brenan, *A Life of One's Own* (London, Jonathan Cape, 1962), p. 236

44 Xan Fielding (ed.), *Best of Friends: The Brenan-Partridge Letters* (London, Chatto and Windus, 1986), p. 3

45 Carrington to Lytton Strachey, 14 May 1921, in Garnett, pp. 177–8

46 Lytton Strachey to Carrington, 20 May 1921, ibid., pp. 182–3

47 Carrington to Noel Carrington, 10 October 1922, Texas

Chapter 5

1 Carrington to Gerald Brenan, 19 October 1924, in Garnett, p. 304

2 Garnett, *The Flowers of the Forest*, p. 107

3 Enid Marx and Margaret Lambert, *Popular Art* (Reading, Museum of English Rural Life, 1958)

4 Carrington to Lytton Strachey, 24 November 1920, in Garnett, p. 171

5 Carrington to Noel Carrington, 15 July 1921, ibid., p. 188

6 Carrington to Gerald Brenan, 5 July 1921

7 Carrington to Lytton Strachey, 15 February 1922, in Garnett, p. 204

8 Lytton Strachey to Carrington, 3 September 1916, BL

9 Carrington to Lytton Strachey, 7 August 1917, ibid.

10 Carrington to Mark Gertler, 21 September 1917, Texas

11 Carrington to Lytton Strachey, 1 November 1928, in Garnett, p. 399

Chapter 6

1 Ralph and Gerald met when they had both been seconded to a new unit, the 48th Divisional Cyclists' Company; *see* Gathorne-Hardy, *The Interior Castle*, p. 99

2 ibid., pp. 107 and 120. Coincidentally, Ralph had been on the same staircase as Noel Carrington at Christ Church, Oxford in 1913. Both men interrupted their studies to fight in World War I and resumed them in 1919 (Noel Carrington, *Paintings and Drawings: Dora Carrington* (Oxford, Christ Church Picture Gallery, 1978), introduction)

3 Carrington to Gerald Brenan, 31 May 1923, in Garnett, p. 250

4 Carrington to Gerald Brenan, 15 December 1919, ibid., p. 149

5 Carrington to Gerald Brenan, 5 August 1921, ibid., p. 189

6 Gerald Brenan to Carrington, 11 June 1922, ibid., p. 221

7 Gerald Brenan, *Personal Record* (London, Jonathan Cape, 1974)

8 Carrington, p. 57

9 Carrington to Alix Strachey, 19 June 1922, in Garnett, p. 226

10 Carrington to Lytton Strachey, 6 November 1922, ibid., p. 234

11 Gerald Brenan to Ralph Partridge, 3 May 1920, in Fielding (ed.), *Best of Friends*, p. 9

12 Carrington to Lytton Strachey, 24 November 1920, in Garnett, pp. 170–71

13 Gerald Brenan to V. S. Pritchett, 4 April 1979, quoted in Gathorne-Hardy, *The Interior Castle*, p. 139

14 Carrington to Gerald Brenan, 1 June 1923, in Garnett, p. 253. One of the 'two English artists' was almost certainly Stanley Spencer

15 Barbara Bagenal (née Hiles) and Ruth Selby-Bigge (née Humphries) had married and had children; Brett had gone with D. H. Lawrence to form a community in New Mexico and Alix Strachey (née Sargant-Florence) had given up painting to train under Freud

16 Roger Fry went to a Bloomsbury fancy dress party as a brahmin; related in a letter from Lytton Strachey to Henry Lamb, 16 June 1913, quoted in Holroyd, *Lytton Strachey*, p. 538

17 Carrington to Gerald Brenan, 27 February 1927, in Garnett, p. 360

18 Mark Gertler to Carrington, 17 May 1920, in *Gertler*, p. 180

19 Virginia Woolf to Barbara Bagenal, footnote to letter of 24 June 1923, *The Letters of Virginia Woolf*, vol. 3, p. 51. Carrington agreed. She wrote to Lytton on 14 June 1923: 'I think Simon is quite right in everything he says in his review', in Garnett, p. 255

20 Carrington to Gerald Brenan, 14 September 1921, in Garnett, p. 195

21 Dr George Rylands in interview with Teresa Grimes in *Carrington*, television film broadcast on UK Channel 4, 1989

22 Lytton Strachey to Carrington, 19 July 1920, quoted in Gerzina, p. 161

23 Mark Gertler to S. S. Koteliansky, June 1919, in *Gertler*, p. 172

24 Roger Fry to Vanessa Bell, 12 May 1921, Denys Sutton (ed.), *Letters of Roger Fry* (London, Chatto and Windus, 1972), vol. 2, p. 507

25 Carrington to Mark Gertler, 8 December 1918, in Garnett, p. 118

26 Roger Fry to Vanessa Bell, 18 May 1921, Sutton (ed.), *Letters of Roger Fry*, vol. 2, p. 510

27 Carrington, n.d. (c. 15 March 1923), Teresa Grimes, 'Carrington', *Five Women Painters* (Oxford, Lennard Publishing, 1989), pp. 113–14

28 Lytton Strachey to Carrington, June 1916, BL

29 Carrington to Gerald Brenan, 15 June 1922, in Garnett, p. 225

30 Carrington to Gerald Brenan, 25 July 1924, ibid., p. 296

31 Carrington to Gerald Brenan, 19 October 1924, ibid., p. 304

32 Carrington to Lytton Strachey, 15 April 1919, ibid., p. 132

33 Carrington to Gerald Brenan, 1924, quoted in Carrington, p. 36

34 Carrington to Lytton Strachey, 18 April 1919, in Garnett, p. 133

35 Carrington to Frances Marshall, January 1924, ibid., pp. 271–2

36 Gerald Brenan to Carrington, 29 November 1919, quoted in Gathorne-Hardy, *The Interior Castle*, p. 147

37 Carrington to Lytton Strachey, 23 December 1923, in Garnett, p. 266

38 Carrington to Gerald Brenan, 1924, quoted in Carrington, p. 60

39 Frances Partridge in interview with the author. A miniscule man and his dog walk a similar road carved into the hillside like 'a stripe of ribbon' in *Uplands around Hurstbourne Tarrant, c. 1916*

40 Carrington to Lytton Strachey, 27 August 1923, in Garnett, pp. 258–9

Chapter 7

1 Carrington to Gerald Brenan, 23 October 1923, Texas

2 Carrington to Lytton Strachey, 29 April 1922, in Garnett, p. 211

3 Carrington to Gerald Brenan, 23 October 1923, Texas

4 Carrington to Lytton Strachey, 10 April

1928, in Garnett, p. 392

5 Holroyd, *Lytton Strachey*, p. 986

6 Carrington to Lytton Strachey, 19 September 1926, in Garnett, p. 341

7 Lehmann, *The Weather in the Streets*, p. 211

8 Carrington to David Garnett, n.d.

9 'D.C. Partride Her Book', 24 February 1932, BL

10 Carrington to Lytton Strachey, 2 January 1924, in Garnett, p. 273

11 Frances Partridge, *Friends in Focus* (London, Chatto and Windus, 1987), introduction

12 Carrington to Lytton Strachey, n.d. (c. 1924), BL

13 Carrington's Diary, 17 February 1932, in Garnett, p. 495

14 Carrington to Gerald Brenan, 16 March 1927, Texas. The purple patch came from Gerald's bed

15 Carrington to Gerald Brenan, 30 August 1928, in Garnett, p. 397

16 Partridge, *Friends in Focus*, p. 74

17 Carrington to Gerald Brenan, 3 April 1924, in Garnett, p. 287

18 Carrington to Gerald Brenan, 18 December 1921, ibid., p. 199

19 Carrington to Gerald Brenan, 27 February 1927, ibid., p. 360

20 Carrington to Gerald Brenan, 1 June 1923, ibid., p. 254

21 Carrington to Alix Strachey, n.d. (c. 1924), BL

22 Carrington to Julia Strachey, 24 January 1927, in Garnett, p. 355

23 Carrington to Gerald Brenan, 31 December 1926, quoted in Gerzina, p. 238

24 Carrington to Dorelia John, Christmas 1927, in Garnett, p. 381

25 Lytton Strachey to Carrington, 6 March 1917, BL

26 Carrington to Lytton Strachey, in Garnett

27 ibid.

28 Carrington to Lytton Strachey, 10 April 1928, ibid., p. 391

29 Henry Lamb to Carrington, n.d. (c. spring 1928), Texas

30 Vivien White (née John) in interview with Teresa Grimes in *Carrington*

31 Julia Strachey's Diary, 2 March 1954, in *Julia*, p. 238

32 Henry Lamb to Carrington, 16 February 1928, Texas

33 Henry Lamb to Carrington, n.d. (c. November 1927), ibid.

34 Carrington to Lytton Strachey, 30 July

1924, in Garnett, p. 297

35 Letter from Catharine Carrington to the author, 31 May 1993

36 Carrington to Lytton Strachey, 30 July 1917, BL

37 Isabel Ide in interview with Teresa Grimes for *Carrington*

38 Mark Gertler to the Hon. Dorothy Brett, 13 July 1921, in *Gertler*, p. 207

39 Henry Lamb to Carrington, n.d. (c. 1925), Texas

40 Henry Lamb to Carrington, n.d. (c. 1925), ibid.

41 Carrington to Mark Gertler, August 1916, in *Gertler*, footnote, p. 120

42 Frances Partridge in interview with the author

43 'Carrington: A Study of a Modern Witch', in *Julia*, p. 119

44 Carrington to Noel Carrington, 10 October 1922, Texas

45 Carrington to Gerald Brenan, 22 January 1925, in Garnett, p. 312

46 Henry Lamb to Carrington, n.d. (c. December 1926), Texas

47 Carrington to Gerald Brenan, 15 October 1924, quoted in Gerzina, p. 210

48 Carrington to Gerald Brenan, May 1926, in Garnett, p. 335

49 Henry Lamb to Carrington, 19 January 1926, Texas

50 Carrington to Gerald Brenan, 22 January 1927, in Garnett, p. 354

51 Carrington to Lytton Strachey, September 1923, ibid., p. 259

52 My thanks to Henrietta Garnett for her description of this painting

Chapter 8

1 Carrington to Alix Strachey, 15 April 1921, in Garnett, p. 173

2 Felice Hodges, *Period Pastimes* (London, Weidenfeld and Nicolson, 1989)

3 Henry Lamb to Carrington, 4 November 1926, Texas

4 Henry Lamb to Carrington, 19 March 1925, ibid.

5 Henry Lamb to Carrington, 24 January 1928, ibid.

6 Carrington to Gerald Brenan, 22 January 1925, in Garnett, p. 312

7 Carrington to Lytton Strachey, 5 January 1921, ibid., p. 172

8 Carrington to Alix Strachey, 22 February 1925, BL

9 Carrington to Lytton Strachey, 22 October 1927, ibid.

10 Daphne Fielding, *The Rainbow Picnic: A Portrait of Iris Tree* (London, Eyre Methuen 1974), p. 121

11 Jeremy Penrose in interview with Teresa Grimes in *Carrington*. The Mexican artist Frida Kahlo painted one of her self-portraits on glass backed with silver papers

12 Carrington to Gerald Brenan, 13 August 1927, in Garnett, p. 374

13 Carrington to Gerald Brenan, winter 1927

14 Carrington to Gerald Brenan, 9 February 1928, in Garnett, p. 386

15 'D.C. Partride Her Book', BL

16 Bernard Penrose and Jonathan Mantle, 'Windjammer', unpublished memoir, 1987

17 Carrington to Julia Strachey, late December 1928, in Garnett, p. 401

18 Carrington to Julia Strachey, c. June 1930, ibid., p. 442

19 Carrington to Lytton Strachey, 21 September 1927, ibid., p. 378

20 Carrington to Julia Strachey, March 1927, ibid., pp. 361-2

21 Carrington to Sebastian Sprott, July 1930, ibid., p. 448

22 Henry Lamb to Carrington, n.d. (c. 1927), Texas

23 Carrington to Lytton Strachey, 29 October 1931, in Garnett, p. 475

24 Carrington to Julia Strachey, n.d. (1931), ibid., p. 477

25 'Carrington: A Study of a Modern Witch', in *Julia*, p. 118

26 Carrington to Gerald Brenan, 14 March 1927, Texas

27 Carrington to Stephen Tomlin, July 1931, in Garnett, pp. 471-2

28 Carrington to Sebastian Sprott, 14 March 1928, ibid., p. 389

29 David Garnett, *The Familiar Faces* (London, Chatto and Windus, 1962), p. 46

30 ibid.

Conclusion

1 Carrington to Gerald Brenan, October 1920, quoted in Gerzina, p. 163

2 Carrington to Gerald Brenan, 8 August 1923, ibid., p. 216

3 'D.C. Partride Her Book', BL

4 'Carrington: A Study of a Modern Witch', in *Julia*, p. 119

5 'D.C. Partride Her Book', 1930, BL

Chronology

1893 29 MARCH. Dora de Houghton Carrington born in Hereford 4th of 5 children of Samuel (1832–1918) and Charlotte (née Houghton) Carrington, who were married 1888

1903 Carrington family move to Bedford, where Dora attends Bedford School for Girls

1910 Carrington starts at Slade School of Fine Art

NOV–JAN. Roger Fry mounts 'Manet and the Post-Impressionists' exhibition at Grafton Galleries

1912 Carrington wins Slade Scholarship, the Melville Nettleship prize for Figure Composition and 2nd prize for Figure Painting

OCT–DEC. Second Post-Impressionist exhibition at Grafton Galleries includes British and Russian artists

1913 Carrington exhibits at New English Art Club. Sells first drawing for £5.8s. Wins 1st prize for Painting from the Cast, 1st prize for Figure Painting and an award for her contribution to a landscape show

JULY. Omega Workshops established by Roger Fry (to 1919)

JULY–SEPT. Carrington paints frescoes for Lord Brownlow at Ashridge

1914 Carrington leaves the Slade. Family move to Ibthorpe House, Hurstbourne Tarrant, nr Andover

4 AUG. Start of World War I

1915 Lady Ottoline and Philip Morrell at Garsington Manor, Oxfordshire. Carrington, introduced by Gertler (b. 1891), becomes frequent visitor

DEC. Carrington meets Lytton Strachey (b. 1880) at Asheham, Leonard and Virginia Woolf's house in Sussex

1916 Carrington receives legacy of £20 per annum from Dr Roberts, a family friend

Begins doing woodcuts

SPRING. Carrington takes studio at 16 Yeoman's Row, SW3.

JUNE. Carrington exhibits still life of flowers at New English Art Club

AUG. Carrington and Lytton Strachey holiday in Wales with Barbara Hiles and her fiancée Nicholas Bagenal (married in 1918)

SEP. Carrington moves into the 'Ark', 3 Gower Street. Starts looking for house for her and Lytton

OCT. Brother Teddie reported missing at Battle of the Somme. Publication of *Mendel*, by Gilbert Cannan, an account of Carrington's and Gertler's relationship. Carrington is portrayed as Greta Morrison, Gertler as Mendel

1917 NOV. Carrington and Lytton set up home at Tidmarsh Mill, nr Pangbourne, Berkshire

MARCH. Carrington designs costumes for John Beauty Chorus in pantomime for Lena Ashwell Concerts for the Troops

APRIL. Hogarth Press established. *Two Stories: A Mark on the Wall and Three Jews*, the first publication, illustrated with 4 woodcuts by Carrington

OCT. Carrington cuts title page and letter for *Lucretius on Death*, 3rd Omega Workshops publication

1918 MAY. *Eminent Victorians* published. Establishes Lytton's reputation

FEB. Gertler attacks Lytton in street in fit of jealousy over Carrington; their affair is over

SUMMER. John Hope Johnstone introduces Carrington to Ralph Partridge (b. 1894)

JULY. Carrington tours Scotland with Noel and Ralph

11 NOV. Armistice Day

DEC. Samuel Carrington dies aged 87, leaving Carrington a small legacy

1919 EASTER. Carrington on walking tour of Spain with Noel and Ralph. Carrington and Ralph become lovers and Ralph a frequent visitor to Tidmarsh from Oxford

MAY. Carrington meets Gerald Brenan (b. 1894), Ralph's best friend, who lives in Spain. They begin to correspond

JULY. Noel, Ralph and Carrington spend fortnight in Welcombe, Cornwall

SUMMER. Picasso and Derain in London for opening of *La Boutique Fantasque*. Derain praises Carrington's painting

1920 Alix Sargant-Florence marries James Strachey

APRIL. Carrington, Ralph and Lytton visit Gerald Brenan in Yegen, Granada

Ralph and Carrington take on 1st floor flat in James Strachey's house at 41 Gordon Square, for trial period, with weekends at Tidmarsh

OCT. Ralph down from Oxford, joins the Hogarth Press (to 1923). Carrington sends 3 pictures for exhibition

1921 Publication of Lytton Strachey's *Queen Victoria*

APRIL. Carrington exhibits *Annie* at the International

MAY. Fry selects Carrington's painting of *Tulips* for the 'Nameless' exhibition at the Grosvenor Galleries

21 MAY. Carrington marries Ralph Partridge. Honeymoon in Venice, joined by Lytton for 2nd week and they tour Italy

JULY. Gerald visits Tidmarsh and intimacy with Carrington begins

AUG. Carrington, Gerald and Ralph spend month at Watendlath Farm, Cumberland

NOV. *Crome Yellow* published, Aldous Huxley's satire on Garsington. Mary Bracegirdle based on Carrington. Carrington submits work to Grosvenor Galleries. Paints signboards

1922 Ralph meets Frances Marshall at the Birrell & Garnett bookshop

FEB. Carrington and Ralph visit Austria with James and Alix Strachey

MARCH. Ralph and Gerald visit Bonamy and Valentine Dobrée in Larrau, French Pyrenees. Ralph begins affair with Valentine

MAY. Brenan at Tidmarsh. Nature of Carrington and Brenan's mutual feelings becomes public, but affair unconsummated. Gerald returns to Spain and Ralph forbids Carrington to correspond with Gerald until November

1923 JAN. Carrington, Ralph and Lytton sail to Tunis from Marseilles

JUNE. Carrington meets Henrietta Bingham

AUG. Carrington and Barbara Bagenal holiday in France at Vermenton on the Yonne, while Lytton attends a conference. Carrington visits Louvre when in Paris

OCT. Ham Spray found within Wiltshire but facing the Hampshire Downs

DEC. Carrington and Ralph visit Brenan in Spain. Reconciliation complete. Returning through France they are joined by Frances Marshall who is in love with Ralph, and Carrington acts as chaperone

Carrington begins tinselled paintings on glass and sells them through Birrell & Garnett bookshop

1924 JAN. Lytton and Ralph purchase Ham Spray. They move there in July with Carrington

1925 Carrington's friends now mostly live in the vicinity of Ham Spray: Dorelia John, Henry Lamb, Rosamond Lehmann, Julia Strachey and Stephen Tomlin

JULY. Lytton's play *The Son of Heaven* (1912) performed at the Scala theatre, London. Carrington paints the costumes

1926 Frances Marshall moves into 41 Gordon Square, so Ralph can join her there

1927 AUG. Carrington goes to Munich with James and Alix Strachey

Lytton rents front ground-floor room at 41 Gordon Square. By November he is in love with Roger Senhouse

1928 JAN. Carrington starts decoration of George Rylands' room at King's College, Cambridge

Carrington's affair with Brenan is over. She meets Beakus Penrose

Publication of Lytton Strachey's *Elizabeth and Essex*

MAY. Carrington and Lytton go to Aix-en-Provence

1929 Carrington, Lytton, Ralph and Sebastian Sprott holiday in Holland

AUG. Film – *Dr Turner's Mental Home* – made at Ham Spray

SEPT. Carrington goes to Côte d'Or, France, nr Saulieu, Martigues, with Augustus and Dorelia John

NOV. Carrington pregnant by Beakus Penrose and has an abortion

1930 MARCH. Augustus John persuades Carrington to exhibit 2 paintings at Salisbury Picture Gallery

APRIL. Gertler marries Marjorie Hodgkinson (b. 1901)

Gerald Brenan engaged to American poet Gamel Woolsey

1931 MAY. Carrington with Beakus on *S.V. Sans Pareil*, Falmouth to Brixham

OCT. Carrington's last painting – *tromp l'oeil* window for Bryan and Diana Guinness

NOV. Lytton becomes ill

1932 21 JAN. Lytton dies, aged 52. Carrington attempts suicide a few hours earlier

10 MARCH. Carrington commissioned by Woolfs to illustrate Julia Strachey's novel *Cheerful Weather for the Wedding*

11 MARCH. Carrington, aged 38, shoots herself

Index

Figures in italics refer to captions.

Achilles 42
Adam and Eve 48, 96
Aeolian Hall 26
Aix-en-Provence, France 110
Alexander, Catharine *see* Carrington
Alpujarras, Spain 86
Andalucia, Spain 81
Angelico, Fra 18, 19, 92
Ann Veronica 26
Annie in a pinny 61
Annie Stiles 61, 62, 63, 75
Anrep, Boris 84, 96, 97, 99, 99, 123
Anrep, Helen 129
Anthony and Cleopatra 95
Apes of God, The 7
Art 19
Ashridge House, nr Berkhamsted, Herts 22–3, 48
Asheham House, nr Lewes, Sussex 30, 37
Ashford, Daisy 48, 64
Athenaeum 18, 84
Audubon, J. J. 54, 123
Austen, Jane 92, 95, 131
Austria 68

Back to Methuselah 34
Bagenal, Barbara (née Hiles) 15, 15, 19, 36, 37, 39, 65, 68, 88, 123
Ballet Russe 57
Balthus, Balthasar Klossowski de Rola 68
Banting, John 94
The barque Harmony 119, 124
Beardsley, Aubrey 19, 20, 35
Bedales School 110
Bedford 14, 22, 26, 28
Bedford Market 14, 17, 18
Bedford School for Girls 11, 11
Beeny Dogs 70, 71, 104
Beeny Farm, Cornwall 71
Bell, Clive 19, 30, 34

Bell, Vanessa (née Stephen) 31, 37, 42, 56, 64, 65, 85
Bellini, Giovanni 68
Berenson, Bernard 18
Bewick, Thomas 41
Biddesden House 128, 129, 132
Bingham, Henrietta 100, 102
Birrell & Garnett bookshop 54, 110, 121
Black Swan 39, 71
Blake, William 19, 86, 100
Bloomsbury Group 29, 31, 56, 64, 91
Bonnard, Pierre 121
Bon Voyage 124, 125
Boot Boy, The 28, 29, 50
Borough Polytechnic, London 37
Boswell, James 67
La Boutique Fantasque 85
Brenan, Gerald 9, 23, 29, 62, 66, 84, 84, 91, 95, 107, 108
describes Carrington's letters 33; gifts for Carrington 54, 94, 97, 130; on Ralph Partridge 64; affair with Carrington 81, 82, 83–4, 85, 100, 123–4; philosophy of love 82; life in Spain 81, 86, 87; at Watendlath 82; portraits of 82, 76; at Larrau 87–8
Brett, Hon. Dorothy 10, 15, 15, 47, 61, 121
Brett, Reginald Baliol, 2nd Viscount Esher 15, 26
Bridgeman, Mrs 63
British Museum 19, 41, 56
Brontë, Emily 131
Brook, Willoughby de 26
Brooke, Rupert 20
Brown, Professor Frederick 9, 10, 12, 14, 19
Brownlow, Lord 22
Bruegel, Pieter 28
Burlington Fine Arts 121
Burlington Magazine 18, 38
Bussy, Jane (Janie) 106
Bussy, Simon 84, 85
Butler, Samuel 26, 66

Cambridge University 31
King's College 126, 126
Campbell, Joseph 88
Le Cannet, France 121
Carrington (Mark Gertler) 21
Carrington (Henry Lamb) 131
Carrington, Catharine (née Alexander) 104, 105, 106
Carrington, Charlotte (née Houghton) 11, 16, 17, 37
Carrington, Dora de Houghton

Life
background and family life 11, 14, 15, 16, 17, 25, 26, 28, 37
appearance 11, 13, 15, 20, 31, 35, 39, 97, 99, 106–7, 131
characteristics 13, 29, 31, 35, 91
education 15, 31, 34, 35, 42, 45, 68
letter writing 7, 9, 32–4
friendships 9, 13, 15, 20–22, 35, 61, 91, 129
relationship with Mark Gertler 15, 20–21, 29, 100
at Garsington 35–6, 36, 40
relationship with Lytton Strachey 7, 29–31, 35, 41–2, 47, 62, 64, 82–3, 91, 131–2
at Tidmarsh Mill *see* Tidmarsh Mill
legacy received on death of father 85
relationship with Ralph Partridge 9, 64, 81, 82, 83, 85, 131, 133
relationship with Gerald Brenan 81, 82, 83–4, 85, 100, 123–4
triangular relationships 45, 64, 82
sapphism 100, 103, 130
portraits of 15, 21, 131
self-portrait 17, 18
self-portraits in letters 26, 30, 31, 32, 33, 41, 41, 42, 43, 81, 85, 108
photographs of 2, 10, 11, 12, 21, 31, 36, 40, 65, 94, 96, 98, 100, 109, 132
portrayed in fiction 7, 33, 35, 92
at Ham Spray *see* Ham Spray
friendship with Henry Lamb 84, 91, 104, 106, 127

travel 68, 81, 82, 85–6, 87–8, 94, 110, 124, 127
relationship with Beakus Penrose 9, 123–4, 126, 131
death 7, 131–3

Art
early work 12, 17
prizes 11, 14, 21, 26
artistic background (*see* Slade) and influences 18, 19, 21, 22, 28, 41, 61, 63, 82, 86, 99, 100, 123, 129
way of working 23, 41, 58, 63, 87, 104, 107, 110, 121, 127
studios 25, 48, 96, 104
commissions 8, 22, 26, 37, 38, 43, 45, 54, 63
love of painting 20, 42, 83, 85, 87, 88
as colourist 63, 88, 89
on being a female creator 12, 43, 83, 85, 131
confidence 13, 32, 34, 37, 41, 129
diffidence 23, 37, 64, 84, 104, 129
appreciation of work 22, 42, 85, 106, 107, 121, 129
fears 131
exhibiting 8, 23, 25, 61, 84, 85, 111
retrospective exhibitions 7, 65
criticism of modern art 25, 64, 84
appreciation of English art 19, 22, 28, 41, 66, 84, 85
teaching 26
fresco and tempera painting 22–3
mural 36, 127, 129
love of the country and country life 22, 23, 26, 48, 65, 66, 71, 91
landscape painting 22, 23, 27, 28, 37, 61, 71, 81, 82, 86, 87, 88, 89, 91, 108–9
figure compositions 36, 37, 45, 58, 59, 99, 100, 110
portrait painting 28, 29, 31, 32, 36, 61–4, 82, 87, 97, 99, 100, 103, 104, 106, 107, 112
Omega Workshops 37–9
book illustrations 41, 43, 43, 45, 45

bookplates 39, 41, 41, 42, 42, 43, 71, 96
woodcuts 9, 33, 38, 38–9, 41–5, 41, 42, 43, 45, 62, 67, 68, 71, 86, 88, 96
letter drawings 9, 26, 30, 31, 32, 33, 33, 34, 41, 42, 47, 59, 67, 81, 85, 92, 94, 99, 108
popular art: canal boat painting 71; circus 66, 68, 70; fairground 66, 68, 75; folk art 65; frames 68, 121; music hall; naive art 84; primitive art 18, 19, 65; scrimshaw 71
signboard painting 9, 66, 66, 67, 67
quilt making 95–6
tile painting 66, 71, 71, 72, 94
still lifes 37, 71, 104
vanitas and flower paintings 54, 57, 92, 93, 111, 112, 123
designs and decorations: 27, 48, 68, 126, 126, 127, 129
glass painting 54, 57, 93, 112, 119, 121, 121, 123, 123, 124, 124, 125, 129
sketchbooks 37, 87, 99
love of theatre 68, 129, 130
costume 39, 130
trompe l'oeil painting 95, 128, 129

Carrington, Edward ('Teddie') 15, 16, 17, 124
Carrington, Lottie Louise 17
Carrington, Noel 9, 33, 37, 38
champion of Carrington's work 8, 65; portrait of 16, 17; sends prints from France 41; commissions illustrations for Don Quixote 45; on holiday with Carrington 63; sends shawls from India 106
Carrington, Samuel (father) 12
background 15, 17, 28, 48; relationship with Carrington 15, 17, 28, 62; portraits of 16, 28, 29, 29, 63; death and legacy to Carrington 85
Carrington, Sam (brother) 17
Catharine Alexander 104, 105, 106
Cattle by a Pond 108
Cedar Tree in Burgess's Backfield, Tidmarsh 61
Cervantes Saavedra, Miguel de 45
Cézanne, Paul 9, 19, 28, 61, 68, 89, 100
Chaplin, Charlie 33
Charleston Farm House, Firle, Sussex 39, 56, 91
Chatalet, Madame du 41
Cheerful Weather for the Wedding 43

Chekhov, Anton 130
Chiron and a Pupil 42
Cholesbury, Bucks 20
Christ Church Picture Gallery, Oxford 7, 65
Circus Horses 70
Clare, John 65
Clark House, Boston, Mass. 65
Cobbett, William 27
Cockney Picnic, A 17
Coker, Mr 107
Colour Magazine 18, 25
Coombe Bissett, Wilts 127
Combe House, Hants 48
Conder, Charles 35
conscientious objectors 35
Cook and the Cat, The 128
Côte d'Or, France 88
Courbet, Gustave 21
Crome Yellow 7, 35
cubism 19
Cynical Age and Youth 42, 43

Daddie and Teddie 16
Dahlias 111, 112, 121
Dahlias (unfinished) 111
Dante's Inferno 17
David Garnett 52, 61
Davies, W. H. 25
Debenham, Marjorie 23
Derain, André 85
Devis, Arthur 68
Diaghilev, S. P. 38, 85
Dial House, Littlehampton 71
Discobolus 13
Disney, Walt 33
Dobrée, Bonamy 82
Dobrée, Valentine 82
Donne, John 20
Don Quixote 43, 45
Doomsday Book 35
Doré, Gustave 86
Dostoevsky, F. M. 20
Doucet, Henri 58
Douglas, Norman 126
Downey Hill 109
Downs from Ham Spray in winter 90, 109, 110
Dr Turner's Mental Home 130
Dying Slave 13

East India Company 15
Eccles, Lord 7
Eleanor, West Wittering, Sussex 37
Elford, Mrs 69, 71

Elizabeth I 28, 63, 131
Eminent Victorians 47, 107
Esher, Lord see Brett
exhibitions
Manet and the Post-Impressionists 9, 19
Second Post-Impressionist exhibition: British, French and Russian artists 19
Ideal Home exhibition 38
Nameless Exhibition of Modern British Painting 38, 85, 112

Fairground at Henley Regatta 68, 75
Falmouth, Cornwall 124
Fancy Ancestors 71
Farm at Watendlath (Tate) 76, 82
Farm at Watendlath 82, 83
The Feetbathers 59, 99–100, 117
Festival of Britain 65
Fishing Boat in the Mediterranean 88–9, 115
Fishing Village in the Mediterranean 88, 89
Flagellation of St Anthony 87
Fletcher, Fanny 54
Flowering cactus 112, 112
Flowerpiece 119
Flowers and drapes 129
Forest, Alaric de 26
Forster, E. M. 106
Fortnum & Mason 121
Fothergill, John 66
Frances Penrose 121
Frank Prewett 52
Fraser-Simson, H. 39
French art 11, 15, 19, 64, 67, 84, 85
French Boys 88
Fry, Roger
as teacher 12, 18, 19, 58; exhibitions 9, 19, 85; Omega Workshops 37–9; as critic of Carrington 56; Carrington's admiration for 85; criticism of 84, 104
Fry bequest 38, 58
Fryern Court, nr Fordingbridge, Hants 103, 127
futurism 19

Gainsborough, Thomas 71, 112
The Gamekeeper's Sons 99
Garnett, David (Bunny) 7, 36, 39, 39, 52, 58, 61, 65, 86, 92, 130, 132
Garsington Manor, Oxon 35–6, 36, 40

Gathorne-Hardy, Jonathan 82
Gauguin, Paul 19, 121
Gerald Brenan at Larrau 76
Gertler, Mark 10, 21, 28, 37, 39, 84
relationship with Carrington 15, 20–21, 29, 100; on Carrington's work 22, 25, 61, 85, 106; affinity in their work 56, 63, 64; described 20, 25; on modern art 19, 84; at Garsington 35, 36
Gilman, Harold 19
Gimson, E. W. 37
Giorgione 86
Giotto 18, 19, 22, 61, 100, 129
Glanvilla, Bartholomaeus de 41
Glenavy, Lady Beatrice (née Elvery) 39
Goblin Market 130
Goya, Francisco de 61, 86, 103, 107
Graeco-Roman sculpture 13
Grafton Galleries, London 19
Graham, Harry 39
Granada, Spain 82, 86
Grant, Duncan 65
defender of Carrington's reputation 7; his paintings chosen by Carrington 54, 56, 93; at Asheham 30; at Garsington 35, 36; director of Omega Workshops 37; member of the Bloomsbury Group 64, 84, 85
Greco, El 63, 82, 86, 87, 91
Greek vase painting 19
Green Mansions 68
Greyhound, The 66, 66
Guinness, Bryan 129
Guinness, Diana 129
Gypsie Horse Stealers, The 68
gypsy tribes 19, 25

Hammam-Meskoutine 86
Hampton Court Palace 38
Ham Spray House, nr Hungerford, Wilts
described 9, 91, 92, 92, 103, 112; decorations and furnishings at 91–7, 106; way of life at 91, 95, 107; views from 90, 92, 94; conversation pieces at 99, 99; guests at 100, 104, 130; photographs taken at 2, 94, 95, 96, 97, 98, 109
Hamnett, Nina 20
Henderson, Faith (née Bagenal) 39, 47, 121, 123, 127
Henrietta Bingham 100, 102
High Wind in Jamaica, A 91

Hill in Snow at Hurstbourne Tarrant
27, 27
Hiles, Barbara *see* Bagenal
Hireling Shepherd, The 22, 28
HMV Gramophone 115
Hoeing 22, 48
Hogarth, William 67
Hogarth Press 39, 42, 45, 68, 110
Hokusai, Katsushika 123
Honey label 39
Hope Johnstone, John 64, 81
Houghton, Charlotte *see* Carrington
Humphries, Ruth (later Selby-
   Bigge) 15, 15
Hudson, W. H. 68
Hughes, Richard 91
Hunt, William Holman 22
Hunt, The 71
Hunters in the Snow, The 28
Hutchinson, Mary 30
Hutchinson, St John 41
Huth, Major 92
Huxley, Aldous 7, 35

Ibsen, Henrik 91
Ibthorpe House, Hurstbourne
   Tarrant, Hants 26, 27
Icarus 88
impressionism 19
Ingres, J. A. D. 14, 18
International, The 61
Italian art 18
   Florentine: 18, (*see* Giotto);
   Roman: 18, 121; Sienese: 18, 86,
   88; Umbrian: 18; Venetian 18, 28,
   86

Jacob's Room 42
Janzé, Phyllis de (née Boyd) 129
Jarvis, Mr 54
Job's Comforters 32
John, Augustus
   at the Slade 9, 12, 18; bohemian
   lifestyle 15, 25, 26; pictures at
   Garsington 35; pictures at
   Tidmarsh Mill 56; a tribute to 39;
   Carrington's letter to 65; creative
   kinship with 19, 84; travelling
   with Carrington 88; Wiltshire
   neighbour 91
John Beauty Chorus 39
John, Dorelia (née McNeill) 88, 91,
   103, 123, 126, 127, 127, 129
John, Gwen 12, 109
John, Poppet 103

John, Vivien 103, 104
Jugend 18
Juggler and Tightrope Walker 54, 93
Julia Strachey (pencil) 103, 103
Julia Strachey (oil) 106, 117

Keynes, J. M. 30, 106
Kitchen Scene at Tidmarsh Mill 58–9,
   59, 67
Koteliansky, S. S. 85
Kristian, Roald 39
Kühlenthal, Christine (later Nash)
   27
Kunsthistorisches Museum, Vienna
   28

Labrador, Canada 124
Lady into Fox 58
Lady Strachey 63–4, 63
Laing, R. D. 29
Laking, Joan 26
Lamb, Henry
   creative kinship with 9, 84, 109;
   pictures at Garsington 35;
   Wiltshire neighbour 91; astute
   critic of Carrington 104, 106, 107,
   121, 129; house decoration by
   Carrington 127; portrait drawing
   of Carrington 131
Lane, Constance 22–3
Larrau, France 76, 80, 82, 87
Larrau Snowscape 80
La Source 127
Lawrence, D. H. 7, 35
Lawrence, T. N. 41
Le Brun, Madame Vigée 131
Legros, Alphonse 22
Lehmann, Rosamond 7, 33, 68, 92,
   121, 132
Lena Ashwell Concerts for the
   Troops 39
Leonardo da Vinci 14
Lespinasse, Julie de 131
Lewis, Wyndham 7
libertinism 35, 38, 61
Life Drawing 13
Lily 123
linoleum cuts 43
Little Gallery, The 121
London 26
   Bloomsbury: 35, 37, 84, 110, Byng
   Place 13, Gordon Square (41) 127,
   130, Gordon Square (46) 31,
   Gower Street (3) 39, 111, Great
   James St 127; Chelsea 56, 66, 84,
   121; Fitzrovia 26; Fitzroy Square

(33) 37; Hampstead 15, 25,
   66, 68, 69, 123; Ladbroke Grove
   (51) 123, 124; Soho 25, 26, 48;
   Spitalfields 15
London Group, The 25, 66, 84,
   85
London Impressionists 21
London Library 26
London Year Book 20
*Louis-Auguste Cézanne reading
   l'Evénement* 28
Lucretius on Death 38, 38
Lytton in his library, Tidmarsh (oil)
   62, 63
Lytton in his library, Tidmarsh
   (sketch) 62, 63
Lytton in his library, Tidmarsh
   (woodcut) 62, 63
Lytton Reading, Tidmarsh 62
Lytton Strachey 32, 51, 61
*Lytton Strachey and Boris Anrep at
   Ham Spray* 99

MacCarthy, Molly 31
MacCarthy, Rachel 130
Macaulay, T. B. 31
Madrid, Spain 86
Magic Flute, The 26
Mandolin Player 92
Manet, Edouard 21, 103
Mansfield, Katherine 35
Mantegna, Andrea 38
Marchand, Jean 85
Marsh, Edward 20, 25, 85
Marshall, Frances *see* Partridge
Marsland valley, Cornwall 63
Matisse, Henri 9, 19, 84, 99, 100,
   121
Maw & Co. 71
Mecina, Spain 86
*Memoir and Poems of A. W. St. Clair
   Tisdall VC* 43, 43
Men of Europe 39
Mexico 121
Michelangelo Buonarroti 13
Mickey Mouse 33
Millais, Sir John Everett 67
Mitford, Pamela 132
Molière 41
Moravian Mission 124
Morisot, Berthe 131
Morrell, Julian 36, 40
Morrell, Lady Ottoline 35, 36
mosaic 37, 96, 123
Mountain church, Larrau 87
modern movement 19
Mrs Box 63, 64, 72

Murry, John Middleton 34

Naked Maya, The 103
Nash, John 22, 23, 36, 56, 65, 84
Nash, Paul 13, 19, 23, 37
Nation, The 84
Nelson, Geoffrey 69
neo-realism 19
Nettleden, Herts 22
Nevinson, C. R. W. 9, 10, 12, 15, 19
New English Art Club 8, 12, 19, 25,
   64, 111
New Republic, The 34
Newbury, Berkshire 54
Newton, Sir Isaac 9, 19
Nicholson, Winifred 111
Nietzsche, F. W. 20
Noel Carrington 16, 17
Norton, Harry 47
Nude Bathers 100
Nursery door, Ipsden House 68

*Oberon, Titania and Puck with Fairies
   Dancing* 100
old masters 13, 14
Olive Slater 106, 107
Olivia 12
Olympia 103
Omega Workshops 37–9, 47, 48, 59,
   92
   Omega Books 38, 39; Omega club
   38
On the Sands at Dawlish Warren, 59,
   110, 110
Original Woodcuts by Various Artists
   39
Ouse, Bedford, The 43, 43
Oxford University Press 43, 45

Palmer, Samuel 41
Park, Mungo 86
Paris, France 15, 86
Partridge, Frances (née Marshall)
   106, 110, 130, 132
Partridge, Ralph 40, 84, 132
   meets Carrington 64; marries 9,
   64, 81, 85; sees Carrington's
   frescoes 23; at Tidmarsh 61, 64;
   joins the ménage at Tidmarsh;
   described 64; portraits of 64, 94;
   libertinism 81, 82; at Watendlath
   81; reaction to Carrington's love
   for Brenan 82; Carrington's
   feelings for 83; on Carrington's
   confidence in her art 85; travels

with Carrington 86; at Ham Spray 104; relationship with Frances Marshall 110; foils Carrington's suicide attempt 131; at her death 133
Patenier, Joachim 66
Penrose, Alec 71, 72
Penrose, Bernard (Beakus)
  Carrington's last love 9; described 123, 124; glass paintings for 119, 124, 125; end of affair 124, 126; film maker 130; makes Carrington pregnant 131
Penrose, Frances 71, 72, 121, 123
Philip Ritchie 107, 107
Phoenix, The 42
Physician's Visit, The 41
Picasso, Pablo 85, 121
Piero della Francesca 18
Piero di Cosimo 18, 121
Plaster Head 93
Plutarch 64
pointilism 111
Poiret, Paul 100
Portraits in Miniature 34
Post-Impressionism 15, 19, 21, 61
Poussin, Nicholas 84
Pre-Raphaelites 21, 22
Prewett, Frank 36, 52
Pritchett, V.S. 83
Prix de Rome 26
Prudence and Justice 56
Mr Pullins 121

Queen Victoria 83

Ramsbury, Wilts 121
Ravenna, Italy 37
Reading, Berks 71
Reclining Nude 19, 20
Rembrandt van Rijn 84
Renoir, Pierre-Auguste 61–2
Ritchie, Philip 107, 107
The River Pang and Tidmarsh Mill 48
Roberts, William 21
Robinson, Heath 123
Roebuck Inn, Tilehurst, Berks 66
Roebuck, The 67
Rolland, Romain 15
Rome, Italy 123, 126
Rookfield, Surrey 68, 130
Roses 93
Rossetti, Christina 130
Rossetti, D.G. 39
Rothenstein, Sir John 8

Rouen Ware 54
Rousseau, Henri 68, 97
Rowlandson, Thomas 71
Royal Academy of Arts, London 12
Royal Academy School 12
Royal Drawing Society of Great Britain and Ireland 11
Royal Opera House 26
Rubens, Sir Peter Paul 84
Ruskin, John 21
Russian art 19
Rutherston, Albert 15, 15, 26
Rylands, George (Dadie) 84–5, 126, 127

St Helen's High School, Abingdon 26
St Jerome 82
St John the Baptist 37
St Teresa of Avila 62
Salon des Refusés, Paris 11
Samuel Carrington 29, 29, 63
S.V. Sans Pareil 124, 125
Sappho 131
Sarawak, Malaysia 61
Sargant-Florence, Alix see Strachey
Sargant-Florence, May 15, 22
Sassetta, Stefano di Giovanni 18, 39, 87, 111
Scala theatre, London 130
Scarlet Pastorale 20
Schwitters, Kurt 96
scrimshaw 71
Self Portrait (pencil) 17, 18
Self Portrait in a C (woodcut) 41
Servant Girl, The 42, 45
Shaw, G.B. 34
Shearman, Montague 39, 43, 71
Shelley, Percy Bysshe 81, 124
Shepard, E.H. 17
Shepherd in Arcadia 86
Sickert, W.R. 19
significant form 19, 37, 58
sign painters 66, 67
Simpson's Choice 39
Sitwell, Sacheverell 29
Slade, Felix 11
Slade School of Fine Art 7, 20, 25, 32, 37, 39, 58, 66, 84, 92
  influence of 11; reputation of 12; staff at 12; curriculum and teaching practice 12–13, 14, 18, 21; Carrington's drawings at 13, 13, 14; certificates and prizes awarded 14, 21; students and staff 10; association with NEAC 12, 19; Carrington's paintings at 21,

22, 22; antique room 12, 13, 21; life room 14, 21
Slater, George 92, 94, 95, 107
Slater, Olive 94, 95, 106, 106, 107, 112
Slater, Phyllis 94, 95, 97, 99, 129
Son of Heaven, The 130
Sotheby's 42
Souvenir of a Slade Dance 15, 15, 19
Spain 79, 81, 82, 84, 86, 87, 94
Spanish Boy 79, 87
Spanish Woman 123, 123
Spencer, Stanley 10
Spreadeagle Inn, Thame, Oxon 66
Spreadeagle, The 67
Sprott, Sebastian 129, 130
Standing Nude 22, 22
Stanhope, Lady Hester 131
Steer, Philip Wilson 9, 12, 19, 21, 110
Stein, Gertrude 38
Stephen, Thoby 31
Stiles, Annie 47, 61, 61, 75, 107
Stories of the East 43, 68
Strachey, Alix (née Sargant-Florence) 9, 15, 64, 82, 100, 115, 121, 127
Strachey, Barbara 48
Strachey, James 82, 104, 132
Strachey, Lady (née Grant) 8, 63, 63, 64
Strachey, Julia (later Tomlin) 126
  desired by Carrington 9, 100; portraits of 100, 103, 106, 117; Carrington's designs for Cheerful Weather for the Wedding 43; model to Poiret 100; observations on Carrington 104, 131–2; at school with Frances Marshall 110; Carrington's decorations for 127; Carrington's glass paintings for 123
Strachey, Lytton 9, 48, 54, 56, 86, 104, 121
  life with Carrington 7, 29, 64, 91, 108–9, 110, 126; portraits of 29, 30, 31, 32, 34, 47, 51, 62, 63, 99, 99; in photographs 31, 32, 109; influence upon Carrington 29; descriptions of 29, 31, 32, 62, 64, 91; and the Bloomsbury Group 29, 31, 56, 64; reasons for Carrington's love 29, 31, 62, 83; sense of humour 30; first meeting 30; physical relations with 30, 31; obituary 34; at Garsington 35; as mentor 35; shared pleasures: books 41, 42, 126; bookplates for 42; Virginia Woolf as mischief maker

42; literary reputation 47; library at Tidmarsh 54, 57; library at Ham Spray 94–5, 95; bedroom at Ham Spray 96, 97; purchases works of art chosen by Carrington 56; encouragement and appreciation of Carrington's work 66, 84, 85, 111, 129; travels with Carrington 82, 86, 88; on Carrington's complicated life 85; his cat 129; death 131–3
Strachey, Marjorie 30, 68, 130
Strachey, Oliver 47, 48, 65, 68
Strachey, Pippa 64
Studies for portrait of Lytton Strachey 30
Study for The Feetbathers 100
Suggia, Madame 26
Swallowcliffe, Wilts 127
Sydney-Turner, Saxon 47, 99, 130

Tennant, Stephen 92
Three Women in a Conversation 85
Tiberius 96, 129
Tidmarsh Inn, Berks 66
Tidmarsh Mill 56, 61
Tidmarsh Mill, Berkshire 85
  decorations and furnishings 9, 47, 48, 54, 56, 57, 58; life at 30, 31, 64; described 47; paintings of 46, 48, 56, 59, 61, 61; studio at 48; atmosphere and taste 48, 54; garden 56–7, 112; ménage at 64, 82, 83; no longer suitable 91
Tidmarsh Mill and Meadows 46
Tintoretto, Jacopo 18
Titian 18, 28, 82, 86
Toledo in a Storm 82
Tolstoy, Count Leo 15
Tomlin, Stephen 9, 127, 130
Tonerspuddle, Dorset 23
Tonks, Henry 9, 12, 13, 15, 19, 85
Travels in the Interior of Africa 86
Treacle Prints 56, 112, 123
Tree, Iris 92, 123, 126
Tristram Shandy 15
The Triumphs of Caesar 38
trompe l'oeil paintings 95, 128, 129
Tulips 54, 57
Tulips in a Staffordshire Jug 54, 111
Tunis 86
Two Stories 42, 45

Ugíjar, Spain 86
University College London 11

Unsophisticated Arts, The 65
Uphusband see Hurstbourne Tarrant
Uplands around Hurstbourne Tarrant 25
Upper Grosvenor Galleries 8

Vasari, Giorgio 18
Velasquez, Diego 21
Venice, Italy 64
Vermeer, Jan 121
Vermenton 87, 88
Veronese, Paolo 103
Vienna, Austria 28
Vigée Lebrun, Elizabeth 131
Vivien John 103–4, 104
Voltaire, François Marie Arouet de 41, 94

votive art 121

Walbury Cottage, Inkpen, Wilts 127
Waley, Arthur 41
Waley, Margaret 71, 97, 104, 123, 124
Watendlath, Cumberland 76, 82, 83, 84
Waters, Cis 99
Waters, Gladys 99
Waters, Iris 99
Waters, Mrs 133
Way of all Flesh, The 26
Weather in the Streets, The 7, 33, 92
Weight, Carel 110
Week-End Review 34
Wells, H.G. 26, 38

Whistler, J. A. McNeil 39
White flowers in two-handled jug 112
'Wild Group' 9, 15
Wilson, Richard 67
Wiltshire 91, 127
Wollstonecraft, Mary 15
Woman in a Chemise 19, 19
women artists 8, 12, 14, 15, 131
Women in Love 7, 35
women writers 131
Woolf, Leonard 30, 43, 68, 99
Woolf, Virginia
    on Carrington's letters 7, 33; at Asheham 30; on Carrington's relationship with Lytton 31; on Carrington's art 37, 42; on Edwardian England 11; on Ottoline Morrell 35; customer of Omega Workshops 38;

commissions Carrington to illustrate Two Stories 42; becomes haranguing 43; corresponds with Lytton Strachey 47; on Carrington's marriage 81; stipulation for creative life 85; in Carrington's trompe l'oeil bookcase 95
Woolsey, Gamel 83
World's Fair, London 65
World War I 19, 26, 64
Wuthering Heights 45, 45, 59

Yegen, Spain 86, 87
Yegen 'landscape' 79, 87
Young, Percy 25, 37
Young Visiters, The 48, 64